William Sharp

Ecce Puella

And Other Prose Imaginings

William Sharp

Ecce Puella
And Other Prose Imaginings

ISBN/EAN: 9783744686280

Printed in Europe, USA, Canada, Australia, Japan

Cover: Foto ©Thomas Meinert / pixelio.de

More available books at **www.hansebooks.com**

ECCE PUELLA

AND OTHER PROSE IMAGININGS

BY
WILLIAM SHARP

LONDON
ELKIN MATHEWS
CHICAGO
WAY & WILLIAMS
MDCCCXCVI

*Affectionately
to my Friend
George Cotterell*

CONTENTS

		PAGE
I.	Ecce Puella	1
II.	Fragments from the Lost Journals of Piero di Cosimo	47
III.	The Birth, Death, and Resurrection of a Tear	81
IV.	The Sister of Compassion	93
V.	The Hill-Wind	101
VI.	Love in a Mist	111

NOTE.

"*Ecce Puella*" *comprises all that the author cares to disengage from* Fair Women, *an illustrated monograph which he undertook at the instance of the late Philip Gilbert Hamerton, for the* Portfolio Series. *It has, of course, been reworked into this, its essential form.* "*Love in a Mist*" *originally was published, with illustrations, in* Good Words. "*Fragments from the Lost Journals of Piero di Cosimo*" *appeared some years ago, in two consecutive numbers of* The Scottish Art Review.

ECCE PUELLA

To the Woman of Thirty

ECCE PUELLA

"*A Dream of Fair Women*: Every man dreams this dream. With some it happens early in the teens. It fades, with some, during the twenties. With others it endures, vivid and beautiful under grey hairs, till it glorifies the grave."—H. P. SIWÄARMILL.

I

THE beauty of women: could there be any theme more inspiring? There is fire in the phrase even. But, as with Love, Life, Death, the subject at once allures and evades one. It would be easier to write concerning it a bulky tome than a small volume, and that again would be less difficult than a sketch of this kind. Who can say much about love, without vain repetitions? Only the poet—whether he use pigments or clay, words or music—can flash upon us some new light, or thrill us with some new note, or delight us with some new vision. There is nothing between this quintessential revelation and that unaccomplished and for ever to be unaccomplished History of Love which Charles Nodier said would be the history of humanity and the most beautiful book to write.

What mortal can say enough about the beauty of woman to satisfy himself? How much less can he say enough to satisfy others?

"For several virtues have I liked several women": and we may adapt Shakespere's line, and say that for several kinds of beauty have men admired women as different from each other as a contadina of the Campagna and an Eskimo Squaw.

I realise my inadequacy. I would have my readers understand that if I were to write as I feel, I would speak not wisely but too well! Fortunately, I cannot rhapsodise: but for this, I might win honour in the eyes of ladies, and concurrently a very natural outpouring of envy and all uncharitableness on the part of my fellow-men. Personally, I would have no hard-and-fast dogmas. Fair women, be they tall or short, dark or fair, vivacious or languorous, active or indolent, plump or fragile, if all are beautiful all are welcome. You, camerado, may incline towards a blonde, with hair touched with gold and eyes haunted by a living memory of the sky, small of stature, and with hands seductively white and delicate: I, on the other hand, may prefer a brunette, with hair lovely with the dusk and fragrance of twilight, with eyes filled with strange lights and depths of shadow, tall, lissom, and with the nut-brown kisses of the sun just visible on cheek and neck, and bonnie deft hands. Or, it may be, I find Ideala in a sweet comeliness: a face and figure and mien and manner which together allure a male mind searching for the quietudes rather than for the exaltations of passionate life. You, however, may worship at another shrine, and seek your joy in austere beauty, or in that which seems wedded to a tragic significance, or that whose very remoteness lays upon you an irresistible spell. There be those who prefer Diana to Venus, who would live with Minerva rather than Juno: who would rather espouse Syrinx than Semele, and prefer the shy Arethusa to the somewhat heedless Leda. Who shall blame a man if he would rather take to wife Lucy Desborough than Helen of Troy: and has any one among us right to lift a stone against him who would bestow the "Mrs." at his disposal upon Dolly Varden rather than upon Cleopatra?

After all, are the poets and painters the right people to go to for instruction as to beauty? Most of them are disappointed married men. Every male loves three females: woman (that is, his particular woman), as he imagines her to be; woman, as he finds her; and woman, carefully revised for an improbable new edition.

II

In the beginning, said a Persian poet, Allah took a rose, a lily, a dove, a serpent, a little honey, a Dead Sea apple, and a handful of clay. When He looked at the amalgam it was Woman. Then He thought He would resolve these constituents. But it was too late. Adam had taken her to wife, and humanity had begun. Woman, moreover, had learned her first lesson: conveyed in the parable of the rib. Thus early did the male imagination begin to weave a delightful web for its own delectation and advantage. When, after a time, the daughters of Eve convinced the sons of Adam that a system of Dual Control would have to be put into effect, there was much questioning and heartburning. Satan availed himself of the opportunity. He took man aside, and explained to him that woman had been reasonless and precipitate, that she had tempted him before she was ripe, and that he was a genial innocent and very much to be pitied. Further, he demonstrated that if she had only waited a little, all would have been well. But, as it was, the rose had a thorn, the lily had a tendency to be fragile, the dove had not lost its timidity, the serpent had retained its guile, its fangs, and its poison, the honey was apt to clog, the Dead Sea apple was almost entirely filled with dust, and the clay was of the tough, primeval kind, difficult to blend with advantage, and impossible to eliminate.

From that day, says the Persian poet, whose name I have forgotten, man has been haunted by the idea that he was wheedled into a copartnery. In a word, having taken woman to wife, he now regrets that he committed himself quite so early to a formal union. From his vague regrets and unsatisfied longings, and a profound egotism which got into his system during his bachelor days in Eden, he evolved the idea of Beauty. This idea would have remained a dream if Satan had not interfered with the suggestion that it was too good to be wasted as an abstraction. So the idea came to be realised. There was much hearty laughter in consequence, in "another place." Seeing what a perilous state man had brought himself into, Allah had pity. He took man's conception of Beauty—which to His surprise was in several respects much superior to Eve—and, having dissipated it with a breath, rewove it into a hundred lovely ideals. Then, making of the residue a many-coloured span in the heavens, He sent these back to Earth, each to gleam thenceforth with the glory of that first rainbow.

It is a fantasy. But let us thank that Eastern poet. Perhaps, poor dreamer, he went home to learn that unpunctual spouses must expect reproaches in lieu of dinner, or even, it may be, to find that his soul's Sultana had eloped with a more worldly admirer of Eve. Zuleika, if he found her, perhaps he convinced. For us he has put into words, with some prolixity and awkwardness no doubt, what in a vague way we all feel about the beauty of women.

For in truth there is no such abstraction as Womanly Beauty. Instead, there is the beauty of women.

Every man can pick and choose. There are as many kinds of women as there are of flowers: and all are beautiful, for some quality, or by association. It is well to admire every type. Companionship with the individual will thus be rendered more pleasing! As the late Maxime du Camp said somewhere: " In the matter of admiration, it is not bad to have several maladies." There are men who, in this way, are chronic invalids. Women are very patient with them.

I do not agree with an acquaintance of mine who avers that his predilections are climatic in their nature. If he is in Italy he loves the Roman contadina, or the Sicilian with the lissom Greek figure; if in Spain, he thinks flashing black eyes and coarse hair finer than the flax and sky-blue he admired so much in Germany; if in Japan, he vows with Pierre Loti that Madame Chrysanthème is more winsome than the daintiest Parisienne; if in Barbary, he forgets the wild-rose bloom and hill-wind freshness of the English girl, whom, when he roams through Britain, he makes the Helen to his Paris, forgets for the sake of shadowy gazelle-eyes, for languorous beauty like that of the lotus on warm moonlight nights.

I wonder where he is now. He has been in many lands. I know he has loved a Lithuanian, and passioned for a Swede: and when I last saw him, less than a year ago, he said his ideal was a Celtic *maighdeann*. Perhaps he is far distant, in that very Cathay which I remember his saying was a country to be taken on trust, as one accepts the actuality of the North Pole: if so, I am convinced he is humming blithely

> "She whom I love at present is in China:
> She dwells, with her aged parents,
> In a tower of fine porcelain,
> By the yellow stream where the cormorants are."*

This is too generously eclectic for me, who am a lover of moderation, and a monogamist by instinct. Nevertheless, I can appreciate this climatic variability. I am no stickler for the supremacy of any one type, of the civilised over the barbaric, of the deftly arrayed over the austerely ungarbed! With one of the authors of *Le Croix de Berny* I can say: "Dress has very little weight with me. I once admired

---

* "*Celle que j'aime à present, est en Chine;
Elle demeure, avec ses vieux parents,
Dans une tour de porcelaine fine,
Au fleuve jaune où sont les cormorans.*"
(*Théophile Gautier.*)

a Granada gipsy whose sole costume consisted of blue slippers and a necklace of amber beads."

Nowadays, we have to admire the nude only in sculpture, and that antique. M. Bérenger in Paris, Mr. Horsley, R.A., and a Glasgow bailie have said so.

Well, well, it may be so. But there are unregenerate men among us. Perhaps this new madness of blindness will supersede the old intoxication. Truly, I am

> " Oft in doubt whether at all
> I shall again see Phœbus in the morning,
> Or a white Naiad in a rippling stream—"

but I have no doubt whatever that others will. Meanwhile we can dream of youth: the youth of the past, the eternal youth, and the hourlong youth we have known ourselves. It is one of the sunbright words. These five letters have an alchemy that can transmute dust and ashes into blossoms and fruit. For those who know this, the beauty of the past is linked to the present tense: the most ancient things live again, and the more keenly. *Antiquitas sæculi iuventus mundi.*

Well, sufficient unto this present is the question of the nude! Let those who will, ignore it. Whatever these may say, there is always this conviction for loyal Pagans to fall back upon—in the words of George Meredith—"the visible fair form of a woman is hereditary queen of us."

III

What a blight upon ordered sequence in narrative, phrase dear to the grammarian, discursiveness is! Yet I cannot help it: to borrow from George Meredith on the subject of fair women, from Lucy Desborough and Rhoda Fleming to Clotilde von Rüdiger and Diana Warwick and Aminta Ormont, is as seductive as the sound of the sea when one is panting on the inland side of a sand-dune. In sheer self-defence I must find an apothegm so good that it would be superfluous to go further. This is irrational perhaps: but then with Diana I find that "to be pointedly rational is a greater difficulty to me than a fine delirium." There are Fair Women, and fair sayings about fair women, in each of these ever delightful twelve novels. Epigrammatically, *The Egoist* and *Beauchamp's Career* would probably afford most spoil to the hunter: but here in *Richard Feverel* is the quintessential phrase for which we wait. "*Each woman is Eve throughout the ages.*"

This might be the motto for every Passionate Pilgrim. For, truly, to every lover the woman of his choice is another Eve. He sees in her the ideal prototype. It is well that this is so: otherwise there would be no poetry, no fiction, and scarce any emotional literature save passionate Malthusian tractates!

But now let me be frank. Out of all the pictured fair women I have ever seen is there one who has embodied my ideal of womanly beauty? This is a question that most of us put to ourselves, with the same apparent arrogance, as if any one individual's opinion had the least value for others, or had anything to do with the Beauty of Woman.

No. Though, in pictures, I have seen a few beautiful, and many lovely, and scores of comely and handsome women, in no instance did I encounter one of whom in any conceivable circumstances I could say "*There: she* is my Eve, past, present, and for ever!"

"I am always waiting," wrote Amiel, "for the woman and the work which shall be capable of taking entire possession of my soul, and of becoming my end and aim." Yes, with Stendhal, we all wait: and one man in a million is rewarded with "the woman," to one man in a generation comes " the work."

What is wanting? Must the glow of personal romance be present before a beautiful woman can embody for us the Beauty of Woman?

> "Araminta's grand and shrill,
> Delia's passionate and frail,
> Doris drives an earnest quill,
> Athanasia takes the veil;
> Wiser Phyllis o'er her pail,
> At the heart of all romance
> Reading, sings to Strephon's flail,
> 'Fate's a fiddler, Life's a dance.'"

Cannot Araminta and Delia be beautiful, though Strephon may prefer Phyllis? Or is beauty in women as incalculable a quantity as the delight men take in women's names? There are names that stir one like a trumpet, or like the sound of the sea, or like the ripple of leaves: names that have the magic of moonlight in them, that are sirens whose witchery can in a moment enslave us. What good to give here this or that sweet name: each man has in him his own necromancy wherewith to conjure up vague but haunting-sweet visions. Equally, if all Fair Women of the Imagination or of Life have names we love, there are designations that seem like sacrilege, that grate, that excruciate. There is a deep truth in Balzac's insistence on the correspondence between character and nomenclature. Still, there are many debateable names. "Anna," for example, is not offensive, yet I "cannot away with it," though tolerant of "Annie." But hear what Mr. Henley has to say :—

> "Brown is for Lalage, Jones for Lelia,
> Robinson's bosom for Beatrice glows,
> Smith is a Hamlet before Ophelia.
> The glamour stays if the reason goes :
> Every lover the years disclose
> Is of a beautiful name made free.
> One befriends, and all others are foes :
> Anna's the name of names for me.
>
> * * * *
>
> "Fie upon Caroline, Jane, Amelia—
> These I reckon the essence of prose !—
> Mystical Magdalen, cold Cornelia,
> Adelaide's attitudes, Mopsa's mowes,
> Maud's magnificence, Totty's toes,
> Poll and Bet with their twang of the sea,
> Nell's impertinence, Pamela's woes !
> Anna's the name of names for me !"

But to return : everywhere pictured Ideala has evaded me. It has been a vain quest, though again and again I have caught just a glimpse of her, a vanishing gleam, a fugitive glance. The other day I was startled by the sudden light in the face of Hoppner's "Miranda," though when I looked again I was no more than haunted by an impalpable suggestion. In the beauty of the flowing drapery, in the breath of that sea frothing at her feet, somewhere there was an evanescent grace which belonged to Ideala. Yet it was not quite hers after all, any more than the indwelling beauty, seen perhaps only for a moment, in the eyes, or revealed in a momentary light upon the face, was hers— the beauty, the momentary light in *Miranda*, in the gipsy-beauty of her of the *Snake in the Grass*, in one or two other portraits of a more delicately refined loveliness, or of the higher beauty, that of the beautiful mind visible through the fair mask of the flesh. Long ago, says Thoreau in *Walden*, "I lost a hound, a bay-horse, and a turtle-dove, and am still on their trail." I think She whom we seek rides afar on that fleet horse, espied for ever by that flying dove, for ever pursued by that tireless hound.

No doubt it is absurd to expect to find Ideala, even among portraits of women who may have been her kindred in the eyes of one or two persons, who could discern not only the outward beauty, but the inner radiance. Moreover, the company is commonly not that amid which one would pursue one's quest. Diane de Poitiers, Nell Gwynne, Mrs. Jane Middleton, the Countess of Grammont, the Comtesse de Parabère, "Perdita," Lady Hamilton, Mlle. Hillsberg, Lady Ellenborough, Mrs. Grace Dalrymple Elliot, and Elizabeth Foster, Duchess of Devonshire, were one and all charming as well as beautiful women. But presumably Charles did not discern his soul's counterpart in Nell Gwynne, nor the Regent Philippe in "la belle Parabère," nor the amorous George in "Perdita," nor either Prince Schwartzenberg or the Arab Sheik in Lady Ellenborough.

In order to judge, one must know. We, who do not know these Fair Women of the past, cannot judge. We must each seek an Ideala of our own. After all, as some one has said, women are like melons: it is only after having tasted them that we know whether they are good or not.

We must be content with some one short of Perfecta. Unequal unions are deplorable. Moreover, it is very unsatisfactory to emulate the example of the celebrated Parisian *bouquineur*, who worried through life without a copy of Virgil, because he could not succeed in finding the ideal Virgil of his dreams. Ideala is as the wind that cometh and goeth where it listeth.

Rather, she may be likened to the Wind for ever fleeting along " that nameless but always discoverable road which leads the wayfarer to the forest of beautiful dreams."

Moreover, She may appear anywhere, at any time. Remember Campion's " She's not to one form tied." Possibly, even, she may be called Nell Gwynne; for to every Nell there will be a lover to whom she will be Helen.

> "Helen, thy beauty is to me
> Like those Nicean barks of yore,
> That gently, o'er a perfumed sea,
> The weary, wayworn wanderer bore
> To his own native shore.
>
> "Lo! in yon brilliant window niche,
> How statue-like I see thee stand,
> The agate lamp within thy hand!
> Ah, Psyche, from the regions which
> Are Holy Land!"

It is a pity that where a Helen is so evident to one passionate pilgrim, she should be merely Nell to the world in general. But so it is; and, alas! the very last person to perceive the connection with Psyche is often Nell herself. Poets get little gratitude, as a rule, for the glorification they effect. Poor bards! they are apt to address as Ideala those who would rather be called Nell, and dedicate their deepest life-music to a mistress who, while flattered, really understands neither the poetry nor the poet, and can be more eloquent over a gift of gloves than over a work of genius. Thus hath it ever been; doubtless thus it shall continue. As long as there are fair women, there will be strong men ready to lose their highest heritage for a mess of pottage. As among the innumerable kinds of flowers where the bee may roam and gather honey there is that flower of Trebizond whose fatal blooms allure the unwitting insect to madness or death, so among women there are some who irresponsibly lure men to sure calamity. Who was the man who said that fair women are fair demons who make us enter hell through the door of paradise? Doubtless *he* loved a flower of Trebizond. Idealists, ponder!

Nevertheless, though we would not naturally seek Ideala among the Nell Gwynnes, it would be a mistake to rise to the high remote air where dwell the saints who have not yet transcended mortality. A touch of sin must be in that man whom we hail as brother, that woman we greet as sister. There was shrewd worldly wisdom in the remark of a French prince, that, however virtuous a woman may be, a compliment on her virtue is what gives her the least pleasure. Concurrently we may take that instructive passage in Cunningham's *British Painters* where we learn how Hoppner complained of the painted ladies of Sir Thomas Lawrence; that they showed "a gaudy dissoluteness of taste, and sometimes trespassed on moral as well as professional chastity," while by implication he claimed for his own portraits purity of look as well as purity of style: with this result—" Nor is it the least curious part of this story, that the ladies, from the moment of the sarcasm of Hoppner, instead of crowding to the easel of him who dealt in the loveliness of virtue, showed a growing preference for the rival who 'trespassed on moral as well as on professional chastity.'"

Women should not be wroth with men because that each male, sound of heart and brain, is a Ponce da Leon. Parenthetically, let me add—on the authority of Arsène Houssaye!—that all the energies of Creation do not succeed in producing throughout the whole world one hundred *grandes dames* yearly. And how many of these die as little girls—how few attain to "la beauté souveraine du corps et de l'âme"? "Voilà," he adds—" voilà pourquoi la grande dame est une oiseau rare. Où est le merle blanc?" "The Quest of the White Blackbird": fair women, ponder this significant phrase. We all seek the Fountain of Youth, the Golden Isles, Avalon, Woman (as distinct from the fairest of women), Ideala, or whatever sunbright word or words we cap our quest with. If wives could but know it, they have more cause to be jealous of women who have never lived than of any rival " young i' the white and red." Yet, paradoxically, with a true man, a wife, if she be a true woman, need never turn her back upon the impalpable Dream; for, after all, it is her counterpart, a rainbow-phantom.

Fair women, *all* men are not travailing with love of you! There are Galileos who would say *e pur se muove*, though Woman suddenly became *passée*, nay, though she became a by no means indispensable adjunct. It is even possible there are base ones among us who may envy the Australian god Pundjel, who has a wife whom he may not see!

Alas, Fair Women only laugh when they behold Man going solitary to the tune of

> "O! were there an island,
> Though ever so wild,
> Where women might smile, and
> No man be beguiled!"

IV

It is not often that picture-gallery catalogues contain either humour or philosophy. There is a naive humour, a genial philosophy, in the prefatory note to that of a recent Exhibition. "As," so the note runs, "there are indeed certain pictures of Women, possibly more celebrated for their historical interest, their influence, or their wit, than for their beauty, some exception has been taken to the title of the Exhibition. The directors, however, do not know of any fixed standard by which such pictures can be judged, and, further, they believe that in the eyes of some one person, at least, every woman has been considered fair."

Whereupon I hum to myself the quatrain from the old north-country nursery-ballad of "Rashin Coatie"—

> "There was a king and a queen,
> As mony ane's been;
> Few have we seen,
> As few may we see."

Alas! there are so many queens of beauty on the walls of picture galleries, and yet one's heart stays secure from any one of them! But, suddenly, I remember a favourite couplet, by Campion,

"Beauty must be scorned in none,
   Though but truly served in one"—

and, having thought of and quoted that sweet singer, must needs go right through three stanzas of his, memorable even in the ever-new wealth of Elizabethan love-songs.

"Give beauty all her right!
   She's not to one form tied;
Each shape yields fair delight,
   Where her perfections bide:
Helen, I grant, might pleasing be,
And Ros'mond was as sweet as she.

"Some the quick eye commends,
   Some swelling lips and red;
Pale looks have many friends,
   Through sacred sweetness bred:
Meadows have flowers that pleasures move,
Though roses are the flower of love.

"Free beauty is not bound
   To one unmovëd clime;
She visits every ground,
   And favours every time.
Let the old lords with mine compare;
My Sovereign is as sweet and fair."

There; all that is to be said about Fair Women, or the Beauty of Women, is compressed into six short lines. This intangible beauty is a citizen of the world, and has her home in Cathay as well as Europe. No one age claims her, and Helen of Troy takes hands with Aspasia, and they smile across the years to Lucrezia Borgia and Diane de Poitiers, who, looking forward, see the lovely light reflected in la belle Hamilton; and so down to our own day. And then, once more, Eve individualised for ever and ever; a challenge to all the world to bring forward one sweeter and fairer than " my Sovereign."

In other words, "each woman is Eve throughout the ages." There are many Audreys, alas —indeed sometimes, within a square mile even, there seems to be an epidemic of Audreys!— but a far-seeing Providence has created many Touchstones. So we will believe that in the eyes of at least one person each woman has been considered fair: though, to be truthful, "a man may, if he were of a fearful heart, stagger in this attempt," as saith the blithe fool of Arden himself.

After all, these clowns and wenches in *As You Like It* are nearer the poetry of truth than that cynical prose of *fin-de-siècle* sentiment, of which this is an example:—

LADY *(looking at a sketch, then at the Artist).* " So:—this is your ideal woman ? "

ARTIST. " It was."

LADY. "Then you have changed?"
ARTIST. "Yes. I *met* her."

As a matter of fact, men who have nothing of the ideal in them are, in the eyes of true women, as a sunless summer. These women, like Clara Middleton of "the fine-pointed brain," have a contempt for the male brain "chewing the cud in the happy pastures of unawakedness."

Women, plain or fair, do not readily forgive. Man should remember this, when he acts upon what he considers his hereditary right to joke upon the frailties of his enslaved goddess. He is apt to think that they are reasonless in the matter of their looks, forgetful that marriage is a salve to all prenuptial display! They do not mind back-handed compliments: they will smile at Victor Hugo when he says that woman is a perfected devil; they have a caress in their heart for Gavarni when he whispers that one of the sweetest pleasures of a woman is to cause regret; and they take a malicious entertainment in the declaration of a man of the world like Langrée, that modesty in a woman is a virtue most deserving, since we men do all we can to cure her of it. But they will not forgive Montaigne himself when he affirms that there is no torture a woman would not suffer to enhance her beauty.

> "Unfolded only out of the illimitable poem of Woman can come the poems of man."

Thus Walt Whitman. But he does not tell us how variously the poets scan that Poem. What would be the result of a plébiscite among civilised women themselves: if they were given by the Powers that Be the option to be beautiful, to be fascinating, or to be winsome? The woman who believes herself predestined to be a wife and a mother will prefer the third: the born adventuress will choose the second: the least domestic will select the first. On the other hand, it might be the other way round. Who can tell? Woman is still the Dark Continent of man. If one were to live to the age of Methuselah, and act on the principle of *nulla dies sine linea*, with every line devoted to the chronicle of woman's nature, the volume would be behindhand even on the day of publication. A copiously margined and footnoted edition would be called for immediately. Even if by that time only one woman were left, there would be prompt need of an appendix. There would also, as a matter of fact, always be a

St. Bernard to grumble: "Woman is the organ of the Devil"—a Michelet to say with a smile that she is the Sunday of man—a cynic to hint that love of her might be the dawn of marriage, but that marriage with her would be sunset of love—a poet to exclaim that she was the last priestess of the unknown.

"Feed me with metaphors," says a poet in a recent romance; "and above all with metaphors of Woman. I know none that do not make me love women more and more."

Did he know his Balzac? Somewhere in that vast repository of thoughts on men and women I recollect this: "La Mort est femme,—mariée au genre humain, et fidèle. Où est l'homme qu'elle a trompé?"

Some day a woman will compile a little volume of women's thoughts about men. These will be interesting. Men will read some of them with the same amazed pain wherewith recently ennobled brewers and the like peruse articles on the abolition of hereditary aristocracy.

Here, for example, is one—

"The greatest merit of some men is their wife."

It was Poincelot, a man, who said this: but let a woman speak—

"Physical beauty in man has become as rare as his moral beauty has always been."

Once more—

"It is not the weathercock that changes: it is the wind."

Since the days of Troy—or of Lilith—men have delighted in calling women weathercocks.

After all, we have been told many times that one of the principal occupations of men is to divine women: but it was a wise philosopher who added that women prefer us to say a little evil of them rather than say nothing of them at all.

V

We are all agreed now, let us say, that there is no such thing as an universally accepted standard of beauty. There is not even an accepted standard of beauty among those who admire the same type. To the most favoured dreamer Ideala will still come in at least threefold guise, as those three lovely sisters of the Rushout family whom, not Cosway, but, like him, one of the finest of miniaturists has pre-. served for our delight. There are a million villages as fair as the one in which we were born, but for us there is only one village. When we quote "Sweet Auburn, loveliest village of the plain," we have one particular locality in our mental vision, as no doubt the poet of the *Song of Solomon* had when he sang, "Come, my beloved, let us go forth into the fields; let us lodge in the villages." Doubtless, too, he had one particular beloved in view, veiled behind his bardic rhapsody. Each of us has a particular Eve behind the phantom of an ideal type.

Of course there are both "villages" and "Eves" that exist only in the mind. There are dreamers who prefer either when most unsubstantial. "Ma contrée de dilection," says the Flemish novelist Eekhoud, " n'existe pour aucun touriste, et jamais guide ou médecin ne la recommandera." Some, too, having found an Eve, will crave for her isolation from the rough usage of the common day, lest she fall from her high estate. They are not altogether foolish who can do so, and can say with a young living poet:—

> "I fear lest time or toil should mar—
> I fear lest passion should debase
> The delicacy of thy grace.
> Depart; and I will throne thee far,

> Will hide thee in a halcyon place
> That hath an angel populace;
> And ever in dreams will find thy face,
> Where all things pure and perfect are,
> Smiling upon me like a star."

This is a temper beyond most of us, who are all hedonists by instinct, and in the bodily not the spiritual sense. Flaubert the man was not representative of us, his weaker fellows. " Je n'ai jamais pu emboîter Vénus avec Apollon," as he wrote to George Sand, when she advised him to try domestic happiness or at least a little flirtation.

Besides, there are men to whom the element of strangeness, of something bizarre perhaps, even of something barbaric, is of primary appeal. The very quintessence, the crown, the aloebloom of this kind of art, is it not Leonardo's Monna Lisa del' Gioconda? Perhaps, even more convincingly, in that drawing of his in the Accademia delle belle Arti, in Venice, of a beautiful girl, with sidelong rippling hair, delicately crowned with vine leaves, with that enigmatical smile on her face and still more enigmatical smile in her eyes—a type finer even than this Milanese beauty? It is a type that does not appeal to many men, but, where its appeal is felt at all, it is irresistible. There is all the seduction of nameless peril in these mysterious faces which apparently tell nothing and yet are so full of subtle meaning and repressed intensity. How else, again, are we to account for the fascination of such an one as Lady Ellenborough, for instance, "the imperious Jane," immortalised by Sir Thomas Lawrence?

Surely it must be admitted that even *his* art does not bestow beauty upon "that witch." Doubtless she had a smile that could unlock prison doors, eyes that could melt a Marat or Danton, a mien and manner, an expression and charm, that made her irresistible to most men. But, on canvas, one can see no more than that she looks like a woman who had immense vitality. The lady's story is certainly a remarkable one. Miss Jane Elizabeth Digby must have been a vivacious damsel, even while still a school-girl, and, in the manner of her time, learning to spell execrably. She was one of the fortunate women born with the invisible sceptre. If she had been an actress, she would have been the empress of the stage; if she had been a demi-mondaine, she would have been the Aspasia of her day: if she had been a queen, she would have been a Catherine of Russia. Again, she was one of those impetuous people who have no time to be virtuous. We know next to nothing of her girlhood, yet we may be sure that she set her nursemaid a bad example in flirtation, and shocked her governess, if she had one, by many abortive intrigues. No doubt her friends thought that she would settle down and be good when she became the wife of the Earl of Ellenborough. They argued that what a high-spirited Miss Digby would do, a proud-spirited Countess of Ellenborough would disdain. But Miss Jane Elizabeth had, she considered, come into the world to enjoy herself in her own way. Not long after her marriage she permitted the too marked attention of Prince Schwartzenberg, and this brought about a duel between that gentleman and Lord Ellenborough. Neither duellist was killed: and the only result was that not long afterwards the lady made up her mind to go off with Prince Schwartzenberg. After a time Lord Ellenborough died, and then his widow married the Prime Minister of Bavaria. That a genuine passion for this strange woman animated the Bavarian noble is clear, not only from his having offered marriage to a lady of such doubtful reputation, but from the tragic circumstance that, when she tired of him in turn, and set forth once more on her dauntless quest of man, he committed suicide. She had several episodes between this date and that when she found herself in Syria, and espoused to an Arab Sheik of Damascus. It would be incredible that she died in his arms in the desert, were it not for the additional fact that she was at that moment contemplating an elopement with her handsome dragoman. Miss Digby was, certainly, not one of those "beauties" towards whom—as Gautier advises—one should go straight as a bullet. Instead of our seizing "her by the tip of the wing, politely but firmly like a gendarme," she would be much more likely to seize us. She was unreasonable, we will admit, but then, with Mme. de Girardin, she might exclaim "Be reasonable! which means: No longer hope to be happy." Obviously she was of those essentially feline women of whom Edgar de Meilhan speaks when he says that "tigers, whatever you may say, are bad companions." "With regard to tigers," he adds, "we tolerate only cats, and then they must have velvet paws." Neither Lord Ellenborough, nor the Bavarian Prime Minister, nor the Arab Sheik, nor any other of her special friends, would deny that a little more velvet on the paws of the sprightly Jane Elizabeth would have been an advantage.

There are always women of this kind, who exercise an imperious and inexplicable sway over the male imagination, or, to be more exact, over the imagination of certain males. It is no use to reason with the bondager. With the King in *Love's Labour's Lost* he can but reply

> "Yet still she is the moon, and I the man.
> The music plays . . ."

We are fortunate, possibly, who never hear this music, a bewildering strain from the heart of the Venusberg. Rather that "silver chiming," which is "the music of the bells of wedded love." Poets are terrible romanticists in the matter of the affections. They are the most faithful of lovers to some impossible She: but they are apt to have wandering eyes in the ordinary way of life. Too many behave, even on the threshold of the Ideal, in the reprehensible manner of Samuel Pepys when that famous chronicler and incurable old pagan found himself in church one fine day. " Being wearied," he writes, " turned into St. Dunstan's Church, where I heard an able sermon of the minister of the place; and stood by a pretty modest maid, whom I did labour to take by the hand; but she would not, but got further and further from me; and, at last, I could perceive her to take pins out of her pocket to prick me if I should touch her again—which, seeing, I did forbear, and was glad I did spy her design. And then I fell to gaze upon another pretty maid in a pew close to me, and she on me; and I did go about to take her by the hand, which she suffered a little and then withdrew. So the sermon ended." It is to be feared that Pepys had not realised that counsel of perfection, which may be given in the guise of a phrase remembered from *Evan Harrington*,—" Both Ale and Eve seem to speak imperiously to the love of man. See that they be good, see that they come in season."

VI

" BUT how to know beauty in woman when one sees it, that is the question," said to me a disappointed bachelor friend the other day.

"If there is no absolute beauty, and if the type is so much distributed in various guises, how is a man who cares only for dark women to see the insignia of beauty in those who have red hair or yellow, and blue eyes, and in the matter of complexion are like curds and cream stained with roses?"

Alas for these uncertain ones, there is nothing for it but a steady course of gratifying and educating the Appreciative Faculties! To my querist I replied in the words of Gautier as Edgar de Meilhan: "Go straight as a bullet towards your beauty; seize her by the tip of her wing, politely but firmly, like a gendarme."

But is there for you, for me, a fundamental charm? That charm, surely, must be distinction. With the Egoist, " my thoughts come to this conclusion, that, especially in women, distinction is the thing to be aimed at." This, alone, is what survives, perhaps all that ever lived, in the portraits of the "beauties" of a bygone day. Then, too, it must be kept in mind that the painter, even more than the poet, is a born sycophant. He loves the sweet insincerities of the plausibly impossible. Most of us are apt to be deceived by the inuendoes of anecdote, the flatteries of rumour, the glamour of the Past, the mirage of history. Take, for example, Botticelli's well-known "La Bella Simonetta," the lady whom Giuliano de Medici made his mistress because of her winsome beauty. "La Bella Simonetta:" there is magic in the name: it is a sweet sound echoing down the corridors of memory. Alessandro Filipepi painted her before the greater name of Sandro Botticelli became a mockery among the ungodly who railed at Savonarola and his teachings. Angelo Politian and Pulci wedded her loveliness to lovely words, and . . . whose pulse, now, would quicken because of la bella Simonetta? Even through the ingenuity of Sandro's art, a quite ordinary damsel confronts us.

Again, take the acknowledged Fair Women of our own country and of a time nearer our own: two types so popular as Lely's Countess of Grammont and Van Dyck's Countess of Sutherland.

While it is easy to understand how Elizabeth Hamilton became "la belle Hamilton" at the Court of Charles II., and had more offers of marriage than the number of years she had lived, till, in the third year of the Restoration, she gave her hand to the celebrated wit and courtier, the Comte Philiberte de Grammont, most of us doubtless would find it difficult to discover that "fundamental charm" we hoped to see. I could believe all that her brother Anthony could tell of her beauty and winsomeness, and have no doubt that Count Philibert was a very lucky man. But, for myself, I realise that even had I been a member of that wicked, laughing, delightful, reprehensible Cavalier Court, and a favourite of fortune in the matter of advantages, I doubt if I would have been one of the five-and-twenty suitors of "la belle Hamilton." Certainly, as things are, one might be Japhet in search of a wife and still not be allured, even in random fancy, by this particular Fair Woman.* Alas, there is yet another charm which allures men when Beauty is only an impossible star; in the words of the anonymous poet of "Tibbie Fowler o' the Glen,"

"Gin a lass be e'er sae black,
  An' she hae the pennysiller,
 Set her up on Tinto tap,
  The win'll blaw a man 'till her."

It was not the fair Elizabeth's "pennysiller," however, that was the attraction, though she did have what the Scots slyly call "advantages."

---

* Marryat's Japhet sought a father, but this is not a misapplication to boggle at!

Nevertheless, it is clear she must have in her beauty something that appeals to many minds and in different epochs. The fastidious nobles and wits of the Restoration admired her; Sir Peter Lely expended his highest powers in painting her; his portrait of her has long been the gem of the famous series known as the "Windsor Beauties," and at Hampton Court she is ever one of the most popular of the ladies of the Stuart *régime.*

Probably the Countess of Sutherland, of whom Van Dyck, it is thought, so much enjoyed the painting, must have been more winsome in looks, as she was certainly superior in graces of mind and spirit. This is the famous Lady Dorothy Sidney, daughter of the second Earl of Leicester and wife of that Lord Sunderland, the first of his title, who fell fighting under the Royalist flag at the Battle of Newbury; not to be remembered for this now, however, but as the "Sacharissa" of Edmund Waller's love-poems. True, Waller, who was for generations one of the most popular, and for a few decades *the* most popular of all English poets, is now almost as little read as the least notable of his contemporaries. He aspired to be England's Petrarch, and like Lovelace with one flawless lyric, or like Blanco White, or the French poet, Félix Arvers, with a single sonnet, is now among the immortals by virtue only of one little song. Possibly Laura had as good reason for discounting the passion of her Petrarco as Dorothy Sidney had for qualification of the prolonged homage of Waller. Both "My deathless Laura" and "My divine Sacharissa" married another person than the lover who gave immortality in verse; married, and had children, and occasionally perhaps glanced at the Sonnets to Laura, or the Poems addressed to Sacharissa. Not only, indeed, did Lady Dorothy choose Lord Sunderland in preference to Waller, but as a widow she even preferred the practical poetry of a Mr. Robert Smythe's wooing to that which in her youth she had had so much experience of in verse. Fair and comely she seems in Van Dyck's portrait of her, though not the Sacharissa of whom one had dreamed. Was it this attractive English lady who was the inspirer of "Go, lovely Rose?" The thought suggests the strange revelation it would be, if we were to be entertained with a series of authentic likenesses of all the beautiful women we have loved or dreamed of across the ages. "A Dream of Fair Women;" what would Helen say to it, or Cleopatra, or Guenevere, or, for that matter, Eve herself? What a desert of disillusion would exist between the catalogue-entry, " Helen, daughter of Leda queen to King Tyndarus, who became the wife of Menelaus, and subsequently went abroad with Paris: commonly known as Helen of Troy," and the quoted motto-lines from Marlowe :—

> "Is this the face that launched a thousand ships
> And burned the topless towers of Ilium?"

Again, fancy the astonishment and chagrin of Mr. Swinburne, if he passed one by one the actual counterparts of the ladies of the " Masque of Queen Bersabe," from Herodias to that Alaciel whose eyes " were as a grey-green sea," and found that he could not recognise one of those vignettes in red or white flame which he wrought so wondrously in the days of his youth! Semiramis, in truth, may have been but a handsome woman with a temper, the Queen of Sheba nothing more than distinctly pretty, and Sappho passionate but plain.

But there is a difference between the praisers of Royal beauty and those who hymn ladies whom they can also approach when the lyre is laid aside. We believe in Laura and Sacharissa and Castara, and many other fair dames beloved of the sons of Apollo. If for nothing else than because she inspired the loveliest of all Waller's songs, we would look with homage at this Fair Woman whom the genius of Vandyck has given us a glimpse of:—

> "Go, lovely Rose,
> Tell her that wastes her time and me,
> That now she knows
> When I resemble her to thee
> How sweet and fair she seems to be.
>
> "Tell her that's young,
> And shuns to have her graces spied,
> That hadst thou sprung
> In deserts where no men abide,
> Thou must have uncommended died.
>
> "Small is the worth
> Of beauty from the light retired;
> Bid her come forth,
> Suffer herself to be desired,
> And not blush so to be admired.
>
> "Then die, that she
> The common fate of all things rare
> May read in thee,
> How small a part of time they share
> Who are so wondrous sweet and fair."

After all, perhaps the secret of our delight in these Ladies of "the glowing picture and the living word" is this: that, even of the fairest, the true lover can say, with the poet of "The Moonstar"—

> "Lady, I thank thee for thy loveliness,
> Because my lady is more lovely still."

VII

To return to the Fair Women of Painting. Here, alas, there remain always one or two unforgivable disillusions. To begin with, there is the inevitable Eve; generally either a matronly person discomfortably garbless, or a self-conscious studio model. There is Helen of Troy, gloriously immortal in the hexameters of Homer and the heroics of Marlowe, but made ridiculous by innumerable painters. And, to come home, there is our own Helen: Mary of Scotland. Is there indeed a portrait of the Queen of Scots in existence which any Mariolater could have pleasure in looking at? There are certain women we never wish to see except in mental vision. Some readers may recollect the Sapphic fragment preserved by Hephaestion, which tells us simply that "Mnasidica is more shapely than the tender Gyrinno." Fortunate Mnasidica, who has haunted the minds of men ever since, through never once having been enslaved by sculptor or painter of any period! Beautiful Shapeliness, that none can gainsay! Painters who give us Helens and Cleopatras and Queen Maries seem to be quite unaware of the heavy handicap they put upon their productions. And so it goes without saying, that all portraits of Mary of Scotland are disappointing, from that of the earliest anonymous limner to that of Mr. Lavery. There is not one of us *blasé* enough to with stand the cruel disillusion of what, by way of adding insult to injury, is called "authentic likeness." Poor Mary! She has paid bitterly in innumerable portraits for the wonderful rumour of her beauty in her own day. No man who respects himself should commit *lèse majesté* by ungracious comment before any canvas of this pictorially much misrepresented Queen. It does indeed make one glad that a few others world-famous for their beauty were spared the ignominy of pictorial immortality.

If all Fair Women of Picture-world were brought together, it would be made quite clear that the one thing which in a thousand instances escapes the painter is expression. Expression is the morning glory of beauty. A few men in all ages have understood this, Leonardo and the great Italians pre-eminently. It is to the credit of many of the most eccentric "impressionists" that they have wearied of conventional similitude, and striven to give something of the real self of the person whose likeness is being transferred to canvas. These, with Bastien Lepage, have realised that "we must change our ways if any of our work is to live." "We must try," adds that notable artist of whom Mrs. Julia Cartwright has recently given us so excellent a biography, "we must try to see and reproduce that inmost radiance which lies at the heart of things, and is the only true beauty, because it is the life."

That inmost radiance! To discern it, to apprehend it, to reveal it to others, that is indeed the quintessential thing in all art.

But the spectator must not only make allowances for the painter of a portrait; he must himself exercise a certain effort. In a word, he must bring the glow of imagination into play, he must let his mental atmosphere be nimble and keenly receptive. He must remember that while portraiture may have verisimilitude of a kind, it can very rarely simulate that loveliest thing in a woman's beauty—expression. He must discern in the canvas a light that is not there. He must see the colour come and go upon the face, must see the eyes darken or gleam, the lips move, the smile just about to come forth : and, if possible, the inner radiance that, in many vivid and fine natures, seems to dwell upon the forehead, though too fugitive ever to be caught, save as it were for a moment unawares.

FRAGMENTS FROM THE LOST JOURNALS OF PIERO DI COSIMO

To E. A. S.

FRAGMENTS FROM THE LOST JOURNALS OF PIERO DI COSIMO*

BEFORE I went to Rome with my master Cosimo many strange things happened. No perilous or untoward incidents befell me, it is true, but I was ever so curious in the byways of life that each day brought me something whereat to marvel greatly. It was ever so with me. Life itself is the supreme mystery: whoso fathoms that will solve the whole secret that has puzzled the wisest men of all time. Yet the more I think (and what a strain this endless thinking is—thinking, thinking, thinking!) the more I realise that there can be no discovery for any man save the revelation that

---

* Doubtless the Journal of Piero di Cosimo, or certain portions of it, must have been known to Vasari. His description, certainly, of the Car of Death, closely tallies with Piero's own.

the world exists for him only. What I mean is clear, though peradventure to some it might seem either a sport in words, an untimely folly, or to others a dark saying, such as the occult wisdom of those soothsayers and astrologers who, I am well assured, play upon the ignorance of the uneducated. It is this: that whatsoever this world has, behind its veil, as it were; such hidden beauty or strangeness or terror is only to be seen of those eyes which bring their own power of seeing. Children and many ignorant country-people believe, that the fogs and rains which the autumnal equinox bringeth do indeed obliterate the stars from the obscured heavens: not knowing that their shining is a thing apart, and as far removed from the vanities of this earth as the virtues of the most Blessed Virgin Mother are from the petty goodnesses and shortcomings of womankind in this world—and most certainly from those of the ladies of Florence, who seem to me to have much resemblance to those flighty insects which hover in still noons and at sundown by Arno-side, having all the characteristics of these, but lacking in the most welcome, that they perish speedily, even if they survive their long day from starsetting to moonrise. But wiser persons, to whom the processes of nature are, in their superficial aspects, not in any wise strange, know well the foolishness of such surmises about the disappearance of heavenly bodies because of the rising of earthly mists and vapours. And so is it with the more occult world of thought. One must have the eye of faith as well as the eye of the body. One must know that there is light beyond darkness, life beyond death, spirit beyond clay, just as the educated know that the same stars which we saw yesternight still whirl their silver spheres through the upper spaces, whether mists and darkness intervene or the equally obscuring splendour of the sun. But over and above this there is a further vision which a few have. This sight brings to the mind and thence to the soul what is beyond the extremest visual ken. Men so gifted are the world's philosophers. They see not merely the fixity of the stars and the mutability of the mists and darkness, but the causes of these obscurities : and they apprehend also the laws whereby the stars exist and scatter their remote influences upon the tides of life, whether these be of the waters of ocean or of the sap in trees and plants, or of the hot or gelid blood in the living things of the world, from the lizard and the callous newt to man himself. And yet again there are some who have a still deeper sight. These are they who are the passionate students of life. But of what avail is it that one telleth unto another his interpretation, if the other understand not also something of the occult meanings, the lost language, of which it is the halting translation? There is no salve to our undying curiosity save that which is found of ourselves. Therefore is it why I, for one, have long sought diligently of her, Madonna Natura—Natura Benigna or Natura Maligna?—my one mistress; and how I shall ever so continue, even as I have done from my youth onward.

My youth! Ah! I was young then when I started with good Master Cosimo for the court of Pope Sixtus in that near and yet far-off Rome. I have already, earlier in these journals, written of my lonely but not unhappy boyhood, but now I cannot help recalling those bygone days. Here is a letter which Cosimo Rosselli, my good master, my very father, wrote to me, now years agone. It is already stained with some chemic dissolution: as the world is with the stain of mortality: as *I* am, now that I am sere as one of those October chestnut-leaves I brought home with me the other day from that deep glade of Vallombrosa I love so well.

'MY EVER-BELOVED PIERO,' so runs the dear familiar hand, 'the tears are in my eyes to-day, and for two causes. This afternoon, after I had finished painting—and, alas! my craft is not what it was—I went forth to sun myself in the gardens of the Medici, having at all times the entry thereto. There, just as I was about to leave, owing to a twilight wind, somewhat premature and cold, coming out of the greenness of the cypress boughs, I heard a sound as of some one sobbing. It had such bitter distress in it that my heart ached. After a brief time of uncertainty I beheld, quite close, and leaning against a very ancient yew, an old man, so wearily a wreck of life that he seemed rather a human-like excrescence of the tree than a fellow creature. But the crackling of a cone or twig beneath my feet aroused him, and he passed at once from the semblance of dismal death to the reality of a yet more dismal life. He was about to make haste away, as speedily as his age and infirmities would permit, and not without an angry and half-defiant irritation at my unwitting intrusion, such as, I bethought me, betokened some rankling memory of better days, when he stumbled over one of the two sticks whereby he aided his feeble gait. I ran forward to assist him, and whom think you, Piero, I recognised? None other than that true and great painter whom you have so often admired, Sandro Botticelli! Ah, how it made my tears well to my eyes. But though he knew me, he would have none of me. I besought him by old friendship, by the memory of our comradeship at Rome, when he and I and Domenico Ghirlandajo, and Luca of Cortona, and Piero Perugino, all wrought together for the Papal award. He laughed once, but bitterly; and taunted me, by asking if I had yet turned my pictures into a jeweller's stock; alluding therein to the method whereby I gained the Pope's prime favour, by the excessive gilding of my work, which made his Holiness believe it to be superior to the productions of better men—(a matter, Piero, I once took pride in, but am now ashamed of): but, on my silence, he turned away as though penitent before an old friend. "*Mio caro amico, mio maestro carissimo,*" I began, when he brusquely interrupted me, and cried "*Ecco!* Cosimo Rosselli, I am Alessandro Filipepi, the son of Mariano Filipepi, of Florence, and have nought to do with the vain dabbler in painted follies whom men call

Botticelli. You knew me of old, and may call me Sandro if you will, but not that other name. Shall my tears and my bitter repentance never wash out those days of sinful vanity!" To the which heart-wrung cry I replied: "I knew you had thrown away brush and pencil, *Sandro mio*, and that you had become a Piagnone,* but I never believed, I cannot now believe, that you, *you*, the master Botticelli—nay, you *must* let me say it—can forget your art. How well I remember your saying to Ghirlandajo, that work was good but beauty was better, as the soul is lovelier than even the most fair body. You cannot have forgotten that, nor how you once told Luca Signorelli that pure colour was like God, for the very being of God is pure music, and pure colour is but the visible and beautiful tranced body of music. Whereupon he sighed, looked at me long and earnestly; then, muttering only, "I am well, I am well, I want for nought," made me sign of farewell, and went on his way. But for hours afterward, ay and oft since, methought I heard that bitter, miserable sob where the yew and cypress shadows were.

---

* That is, of the bigoted sect of Fra Girolamo Savonarola.

'And the other cause of my weeping to-day, though rather a soft summer rain, such as falls from my white lilac (where the young thrush revolves his song oftentimes leisurely, but again with such a marvellous swift joy and sweetness as to make me wonder at God's grace to these creatures of a springtide), rather such a rain I say than the sterner tears which I shed earlier over my unhappy Botticelli.

'For I came by chance, dear son, upon an early and a strange letter of thine, when thou wert not yet in thy fifteenth year. How keenly it recalled those bygone days! I seemed once again to see thee, ever studious, and apart from thy fellows, and oftentimes rapt in strange imaginings. Fond, indeed, thou wert then as now of remote places, and of all things fantastic, and of solitude; a dreamy youth, moreover, wont to reply vaguely to questions of common import. And in this letter of thine, writ as I say when thou were not yet in thy fifteenth year, thou speakest strangely for a youth. "The bale of life is so bitter that one hath perforce to occupy one's-self with such diversion as is offered by the strange, the fantastic, the terrible." What manner of boy is it who writeth thus? Again: "I saw to-day a cloud of those smoke-like balls of seed blown from a field of dandelions: how beautiful they were, how exquisite their dalliance with the light wind, how perfect each delicate part—nothing out of heaven more wondrous light and aërial! All were blown upon a rotting dunghill, amid whose indiscriminate filth and stench were perishing butterflies, and some stained apple-blossoms, and voracious beetles and centipedes and other horrible insects, with worms, unwieldy and overgorged, rejoicing in corruption. And when I went home and fell into a dream, I was sore perplexed whether I had seen all this, or had been but deliberating upon dear ambitions, and fair hopes, and human life, and the end thereof, and the immortality of the worm." Ah, Piero, Piero, as thou wert then, so art thou now; men say strange things of thy wayward life, though they praise thy genius. And the ending of thy letter, how sad it is! "But thee, Cosimo Rosselli, my master, whom I love, can deep affection save thee from the ills of life? If so, thou art saved indeed!"

'And now, dear Piero, though I have seen nought of thee for long, we seem to be closelier drawn one to the other. Wilt thou not come and visit one who, whatsoever men idly say against thee, will ever love thy person as he reveres thy genius. Thou knowest that I am thine in comradeship and love, Cosimo Rosselli.'

* * * * *

They say that I live more as a wild beast than as a man: because I bar my doors against the idle and the over curious; eat, only when I am an-hungered; will not have my garden digged, nor the fruit-trees pruned; will not haunt the streets, or the taverns, or the guest-rooms, nor talk much and eagerly of matters that concern me not at all. So be it. Perhaps the wild beast is none the less beloved of nature than the foolish human babbler. Why should I eat save when I would? Why not be solitary, when solitude is my festival? Why have my garden digged or my fruit-trees pruned, when to me the pleasure is greater to see the branches trail upon the ground, to behold the vines grow in their own way (as the human fool will not do, but persuadeth himself to ancestral follies, and conventions of outworn usage). Nature hath heed of her offspring. She hath birds to feed off these grape clusters, whether they be high and wind-swayed, or lie all ruined in the mould; butterflies, too, and moths, that haunt the sugared ooze upon over-ripe fruit; and flame-like wasps darting hither and thither, with keen knives cutting the purple skins; and the larvæ of many insects, and caterpillars and grey slugs and worms—these hath she all to feed, from my vines, as well as me. I am but one of these: but not so happy, because I think: not so wise, because I hope.

*****

Last night, very late (how white the shining of the moon upon the flood of Arno, and how deathlike the city in its silence, though joys and woes, and passionate hopes and more passionate despairs quivered, like exposed nerves, beneath the cold, calm exterior), on my homeward way from Vallombrosa, I stopped at the house of Antonio del Monte, the naturalist. Walking along the chestnut glades, hours before, and wondering if ever painter would be born who would be able to paint *living* nature, and not but our dull dream of her (yet, in my vanity, thinking of that landscape which I painted for Pope Sixtus, when I went to Rome with Cosimo Rosselli, the one which gained me so much praise and so many commissions): wondering also, in my strange uplifted ecstasy, if in any other world—if such there be, as I shrewdly suspect, among all those stars and planets overhead, despite what the Prior said to me about the evil and perilous thoughts of the excommunicated and already damned—wondering then if there be any more beautiful than this, with with such infinities of mercy and delight for us, and indeed for all living things, I beheld somewhat that struck me as with a chill of fever. Overhead I saw a hawk, motionless as though painted against a dome of blue. It fell suddenly, many a score of paces—how many I could not say: then hung hovering; and all in a moment crashed upon a hen-partridge cowering over her chicks, and spilt the blood from the cleft head upon the wheat-stacks close by. And further, scarce fifty yards away from where I stood, a fierce stoat crept nigher and nigher to a rabbit, which crouched trembling, giving forth a strange choking sob at times, and at the last sprang upon it and drove its teeth into the rabbit's skull. And further, I saw a sparrow-hawk on a fir-bough, tearing a young thrush to pieces, and scattering the bloodied feathers to right and left. And further, I saw a dead and rotten branch fall and crush a white bloom of lilies on the sward underneath. And further, I saw at my feet a small but agile insect, striped like a wasp, that ran backward and sideward as easily as forward, and it waylaid a tender yellow moth and nipped its head off and devoured it. Then a passion came into my heart, and I went away with my soul sick within me. I laughed at the beauty of the world, and cursed the mercy thereof. And as I passed the vlilage at the foot of the hill I heard a man, blaspheming, strike his wife with savage cruelty; and the cry somewhere of a child wailing in pain. And when I told all to Antonio del Monte, he laughed. He said Nature was a beast of prey. And I—I—have loved Nature, have worshipped her! The end of idolaters is death within death.

* * * * *

I remember well—it was after my first carnival in Rome—that an idea of a new and striking, albeit fantastic, masquerade, came into my mind. Yet it was not there but in Florence that I fulfilled it; and many years later. I was in great favour then with the gay Florentine youth, ever alert to novelties as to fierce deeds: they prized me for my invention in designing pleasurable surprises. Of a truth, the masquerades became new things altogether, after my dispositions were approved and carried into effect. Thenceforth they became triumphal processions, with men and horses gorgeously and strangely apparelled, and with wild or joyous music. It was a fine sight indeed, when, along the flower-strewn streets, young men (nude, or with leopard or tiger skins thrown about them, and garlanded with roses and lilies) rode upon foam-white stallions, these snorting through blood-red nostrils or neighing with hoarse clangours that rang against the black marble and basalt of the Florentine palaces! The sun shone upon the ivory skins of the men and the blanched milk-white steeds, and upon the trodden flowers, all red and white and yellow (that gave up an indescribable languorous and most sweet smell, as though the very soul of spring were dying there and passing away in forlorn fragrances), and upon the gay crowd, so brightly and variously clad, and upon the beautiful fair women—many with wind-lifted hair and loosened bodices, and breasts that gleamed like globed water-lilies: the froth and foam, these, of the carnival-tide—laughing, and throwing those deep blood-red roses which are called Hearts o' Love, and wearing cream-hued and scarlet scarfs, twined round and trailing from the whitest of arms. And not less striking the processional array by night. Down the dark streets tramped the white horses, their riders now in gleaming armour, or fantastically garbed like chieftains of the Magyars or of the barbaric East. Two by two the riders went, and betwixt each couple not fewer than twoscore ten stalwart men on foot, each waving a burning torch in one hand and carrying an unsheathed sword in the other, so that it caught and flashed forth a hundred lights. The horses themselves were a sight to see, in their rich accoutrements! Thereafter came a high car, garlanded with flowers and draperies and many rare devices. And all this to the laughter of men and women, the neighing of the stallions, the clanking of weapons, the sputtering of the torches, the shrill shrieks of Greek fifes, and the furious challenging blare of fivescore brazen trumpets! Ay, these were goodly sights, though none equalled my Masquerade of Death, which is none other than the idea whereof I wrote a little ago: and of which men speak eagerly to this day, some with pleasant awe and dainty shudderings, others crossing themselves and muttering of devilish imaginations and Antichrist and papal maledictions.

I made my Car of Death in such secrecy in the Hall of the Pope, that none—no! not one—

saw it aforehand. Then I made all arrangements, not only in mine own privacy, but wheresoever the procession should pass by; and these arrangements included the way itself, for I had special purposes to fulfil. And all who gave me of their service did so under a bond of secrecy, for after a while it became impossible to hide, from some at least of my assistants, either the parts or the whole of my scheme. There were two of my pupils who were of especial service to me, both named Andrea. The one is still called Andrea di Cosimo: the other, a greater than his master, is known throughout all the lands northward of Rome, and even to France, as Andrea del Sarto. He was brought to me by my friend Gian' Barile, the Florentine painter, as a youth of exceeding promise; and I came to love him, almost as the good Cosimo Rosselli loved me. He was ever a Passionate of art, from the days when he spent his leisure hours staring at the frescoes by Leonardo and Michel-Angelo in this very Hall of the Pope where I made my Car of Death. Rumours have reached me in mine old age that Andrea del Sarto, whom I see no more (whom do I see, I, Piero di Cosimo, "the mad painter," lonely as the falling star that last night swept the circuit of the heavens, and flashed into an oblivion of darkness beyond human ken?)—rumours, I say, have reached me that Andrea declareth my Procession of Death symbolised the return of the Medici. This is false. It is one to me whether the Medici feed upon the taxes of the Florentines, or upon those of any alien city. My device was of fantastical delight and a brooding imagination; and I have thought of stranger things still, but have scarce dared even to suggest them.

Thus was it, then, in the height of the Carnival. My great triumphal car, instead of being drawn by prancing horses and gaily decorated, was yoked to black buffaloes, each of sombre and terrible seeming, with horns overlaid with whitest plaster, and with eyes made hollowly red and burning with virulent pigments. The car itself was all hung in black sweeping draperies, gloomful as a starless and moonless night with imminence of rain; very dolorous to look upon; and yet not the less so because, every here and there, painted with whitely gleaming dead men's bones and broad crosses. High up on the car sat the gigantic figure of Death himself, dreadful of aspect, and holding in one outstretched hand his ever thirsting and hungering scythe. Beneath him, huddled round the huge throne whereon he sat, were dismal tombs, blank and awful. Before the slow-moving car and lowering buffaloes, and after it likewise, rode a great number of the dead on horseback, all singing in a trembling voice the *Miserere*. The sight made many quake, and some who laughed broke into sobs. And at those places where, in former carnivals, the triumphal procession was wont to stop for a sweet and joyous singing, and for the interchange of blythe and happy mockeries and good fortunes, it now stopped also; but, instead, the tombs upon the huge car opened, and thence crawled, or glided, or sprang forth figures garbed in close-fitting black, all painted over with the insignia of death, the grinning skull, the long-jointed arms and legs, and all the bones of the human skeleton. These dreadful things moved close one to another; and then, to the drear accompaniments of muffled strains, sang, in a most melancholy music, that solemn chant beginning—

"*Dolor, pianto e penitenza,*" etc.

It was a strange sight. Many, it is said, dream of it still.

* * * * *

After a still evening, and a sunsetting sky of the most marvellous delicate green, with pale lemon-yellow spaces beyond, the weather has changed. I noted how low the fireflies flittered among the under-branches of the guelder-rose and around the bole of my old yew, and how sultry their wandering lights. The voices of the dogs barking in the gardens of Fiesole came down the slopes no more clear and sharp, but as though from afar, and muffled, as in a dense snowing. Nothing crackled in the garden. That strange beast out of Araby or Cathay, which Messer Antonio gave me in exchange for my portrait of him, made a mewing noise, very weird, yet not like any cat or other animal I have known—rather like a mad person mouthing in vague fear. Methought it might be a lost soul. If—if I——

The rain at last! Streaming, rushing, pouring down; the garden-ways aflood; the house-vents spouting forth upon the streets! Most joyous of sounds! Oh, would I were striding along, singing my Song of Death, amid the now wind-furied glades, in tempestuous Vallombrosa!

* * * * *

II*

YESTERDAY I completed a series of drawings of strange animals, similar to those of dragons, and other rare creatures, which I made for Giuliano de' Medici. I have often wondered if, in some far country, a fortunate traveller will not unexpectedly come upon those half-human creatures of which legends tell us. How well I remember going to a wild rocky place on the Pisan shore, in hope to see the golden hair and white breasts and waving arms of those Ladies of the Deep of whom I heard oft in my boyhood: or, at the very least, to catch the delicate sweet forlornness of their alien singing! One night—it seems but yester eve as I recall it—I lay in a heathy dingle, watching the moonlight resting like the caressing hand of God upon the tired earth: and listening to the deep undertone of the ancient Sea, as he laid his lips against the shore and murmured, in a tongue unknown to men, secrets of Oblivion, and dull, remote prophecies. There was an

---

* The following excerpts, all that remain of Piero's Journal, are plainly of a considerably later date than those just given. The postscript by Antonio del Monte is written on the page immediately succeeding that containing Piero's latest entry. There is some further writing below the 'Requiescat,' apparently in Latin, but, save for a few letters, indecipherable.

absolute hush in the air. Now and again the pinging sound of a gnat deepened the profound stillness. Almost I fancied that I heard the serene aerial chiming of the stars. While I lay there adream, mine ears caught the sound of a faint splashing. I thought it was a fish, leaping in silver upon a moongold wave to snap at a wandering firefly. Then as the sound waxed more distinct and without intermission, I conceived the idea that the sirens were swimming landward, and I caught myself listening eagerly for that wild fantastic music which lures mariners to the doom of which no man knoweth the manner or fulness. Suddenly I heard a low laugh. The sweet humanity of it acted upon me like the dawn after a night of gloom. As silently as the doe lifts her head from the fern-covert when she scents from afar off the prowling wolf, I raised myself. *Per Bacco!* was I still adream? . . . I wondered. A beautiful girl ran to and fro along the sea-marge, her ivory limbs splashing far and wide the foam of each long, low, wave. Her hair drifted behind her like the tresses of a wind-blown larch. Her beautiful naked body gleamed in the moonlight, and as she moved hither and thither, now swiftly as though pursued, now with dainty listlessness, I thought that I had never seen aught lovelier. A little cape ran out from the shore, and as she neared it she laughed low again and again: low, and yet so that I heard it easily. It thrilled me unspeakably. There was in it such unfathomable pain, and yet with—oh, such a subtle rare magic of delight! I felt that I could—nay, that I would—follow that low-haunting laugh, and that ideal beauty, even to the ends of the earth, even though I were led into places of death, unspeakable because of their terror. Suddenly she—this thing of beauty and grace—disappeared as in a wave, and I saw her no more. With the speed of a man fleeing for his life I raced towards the beach. Strange that I should notice, and for a second or two halt, because of the shrill sudden cry of an aziola. It mocked me, I thought. But when I reached the shore, nought was there. There was the same vast stretch of the moonlit deep: the same long low wave, for ever breaking in foam out of stillness, like the froth upon a dying man's lips: the same inscrutable silence on sea and land, save for the pinging of the gnats below the cystus-bushes, and the low thrilling monotone out of the heart of the waters. Hastily I ran out upon the little cape:

but no, nought could I see beyond it or close under. Had I, then, beheld one of those mysterious creatures who live in Ocean, and lament a lost humanity? I wandered all night long by the margin of the sea, but heard no unwonted sound, save the crying of a strange bird far waveward: saw no unusual sight, save a furtive phosphorescence which came and went upon the dark surface of the waters, like an evil smile upon the face of an Oriental satrap dreaming of cruel delights. But about dawn I met a haggard fisherman, who stared at me blankly and muttered some foolishness. From him, in reply to my eager questions, I learned that one Mariana, the daughter of a gentleman of Pisa, had recently become distraught because of the exceeding beauty of a youth of whom she had dreamt—because of his surpassing loveliness, but still more because of his visionary immortality, which could not mate with her earthliness. She had passed through Pisa as one dazed, and had been seen at sundown watching the inward—moving tide, and laughing strangely to herself the while. None had seen or heard of her since. But this had occurred many days—ay, weeks—before mine own adventure. To this day, in all verity,

I khow not whether 'twas Mariana of Pisa whom I saw passing like a dream through the wave, or some Donna Ignota born of the moonshine and the sea.

* * * * *

To-night, as I walked in my wilderness (so I lovingly call my garden), filled full as it is with all manner of strange things and desolate growths, I noticed an unwonted flashing of red lights. Ever and again it happened, and once so that I was almost dazzled. At first I thought some rare creature, a lizard or salamander from afar, or it might be some gem or old-time weapon, lay amid the mould; but at the last I found to my surprise that this flashing of light was caused by two or three blooms among a cluster of nasturtiums. One, in particular, glowed like the lantern of a monk in a dark wine-vault. I knew not till then that flowers gave off this mysterious effulgence, though, now I think of it, Suleiman has told me that he has seen something of the kind in the region beyond Nilus. It has made me think. Perhaps all created things give off some coloured emanation. I should like to paint the people going to and fro in the streets of Florence, with all their hidden sins made visible in furtive flashes of scarlet and purple, and wan green and yellow, and bloodied red! *Cristo*, how the Medici would reward me for my pains if I painted *them!* 'Twould be a short shrift then for the hermit-painter, Piero di Cosimo! Nay, but seriously, what if some of us have this quality? 'Twould account for the divers strange and terrifying apparitions of the dead, of which rumour is oft, in the dark hours, so garrulous.

(*On the morrow.*)

I slept little last night, for a deep brooding over the thing of which I have writ above. I have decided to tell Alessandro Bardi that I shall paint him and his Caterina after all. How I hate old Luigi Bardi! The insolence of the purse-proud man! How dared he insult me that day on the Ponte Vecchio?—sneering at me as a madman because I had stood staring for an hour or more upon the marvellous violet lights in the shallow flood of Arno, laughing loudly while I told him that that violet had to be waited for for weeks at a time; mocking with his twisted mouth, "Violet! violet! *Corpo di Cristo*, hark to the man! He cannot even see aright!" Fool that he was! Howsoever, it is true that painters see deeper into colour, as falconers see further than goldsmiths. And yet, because of his ducats, he thought he could obtain a portrait of his son and his mistress from me! No doubt—*si, si, amico mio*—you shall have the portrait—*ecco!* Piero di Cosimo shall paint your son and the twilight-eyed Caterina.

* * * * *

'Tis a month since I have writ aught in these pages. Alessandro and Caterina are both dead: died o' the plague, it is said. I know better.

They came to me. I made that a condition. I painted both upon one canvas. A comely youth, Alessandro: Caterina's beauty, melancholy, exquisite, like an autumnal eve on the Maremma. How they loved each other! Ofttimes I laid down my brush, and once I burst into laughter so loud and so long that Bardi, the good youth, hesitatingly came towards me, as a stag might approach a hyena. But I waved him back, with muttered execrations. Had he gained but one glimpse of my canvas he would have slain me forthwith. Oftener, I simulated great abstraction in labour, and watched them furtively. Her favourite attitude was to lean her head against his breast, and then, many a time, she sang a wondrous sweet song of the Trevisan (whereof she was a native), so that my tawdry workroom became glorified, I know not how. His pleasure was to stroke her long lustrous hair, and to look dreamily into those shadowy eyes of hers, where immortality seemed to brood amid depths of death. She was with child, and oft looked suddenly at naught, in a wild trouble, as I have seen a white hart do at the falling echo of a far-off baying hound. Ah! this terrible brutality of motherhood. It is a device of nature to humiliate the soul, of which she is jealous unto death. She has disguised it in a rainbow, as a Borgia might convey a debilitating, slow-killing poison in an exquisite rose. . . . Well, I watched them oft. The other eventide I was sitting alone, brooding upon the frightful thing before me, all but finished it was, when Suleiman entered. I did not hear him knock, nor do I believe he did, though he so averred. He is a dark and evil spirit. He stared at my canvas, and an awful look lurked about his eyes and mouth. Then he laughed. Thereafter he told me that he, too, bore a bitter grudge against Luigi Bardi. *Dio mio*, how it thrilled me when the swart Oriental —Suleiman el Moro, he calls himself, though hell knows his accursed name—confessed that he had woven a spell upon my brushes, so that demons had entered into them. "To what end?" I asked, with my tongue moving like a wounded thing in time o' drought. "So that when Luigi Bardi's son and his love look upon your painting they shall become what you have depicted them." In horror I rose, thrust the grim saturnine Suleiman aside, and ran from the house, as one pursued by a demon. For I had painted Alessandro as the Lust of a Devil, and Caterina as the Desire of a Beast. 'Twas a wild revenge upon Bardi: but now God had turned it against me. I stayed all the night with Antonio del Monte, moaning so, at times, that he cried to me at last a wolf were fitter company. On the morrow, filled with remorse, and resolved to end my folly, I hastened back to my house. As I passed under the shadow of the Duomo I met Pietro Avante, who asked me if I had heard that Sandro Bardi and Caterina Dà Ru had gone secretly from Florence—so it was said, at the least, for nowhere were they to be found. My heart sank deep, deep, though I put a brave front against disastrous fate. At the end of the Borgo di San Sepolcro my late pupil, Giraldo da Signa, stopped me, and asked me if I knew whither Suleiman el Moro was bound. "Wherefore?" I asked. "Because, as I was going home, an hour before dawn—having been at the carousal of Berto Danoli, who is returning to Venice as the heir of his old uncle Benedetto —curse him for a miser!—I descried El Moro riding upon a white horse, and methought he had the face of a corpse as he stared, in his swift passing, towards the way of the Pisan Gate.' 'I know not, fool,' I muttered; 'think you the accursed Egyptian, or whatever he be, is my son?' But thereafter I hurried with trembling limbs to my house. When I entered the workroom I thought my heart-strings would break: 'twas as though my heart were a wet cloth wrung by a woman on Arno-side. There lay Alessandro Bardi and Caterina, not only dead, but horrible in death: with a likeness, appalling, frightful, to their ghastly phantasma on the canvas. I know not how they died: whether she shrieked and fell (they must have come earlier than their wont, and seized the opportunity to look at my canvas), or whether he turned and slew her and then strangled himself, or whether demons wrought their death, I know not. They looked as though they had died of the Black Pest. Hastily I dashed paint this way and that across my accursed picture, and scraped the distorted features with the palette knife, till it was as ghastly a ruin as the love of Sandro and Caterina. Then again I rushed out, crying, '*The Pest! the Pest!*' At first I was taken for mad. I know not how it might have gone with me; but the authorities, fearing to have even the name of the plague mentioned, sent for, and privily removed, the two dead bodies, and had them burned on a waste spot half a league behind the wester slope of Fiesole. And now it is all over—all gone—all done. It might be a horror of the night, but for this letter from Luigi Bardi, with its awful curse; but for this oily, dull-savoured, blood-red pebble, come to me this morning, whence I know not, without word of any kind, without indication, save the word 'Suleiman' cried hollowly behind me by—by—*something*.

* * * * *

Old age is terrible when manhood is prostituted in it. It ought to be as full of peace and beauty as a snow-covered landscape in sunlight, as happy as a child's laughter among unfolding blossoms. To be a derelict upon the ocean of life is worse than any sudden wreckage. Death itself can never be truly abject: living death is the grave: corruption.

* * * * *

Sorely distraught have I been of late. No sound could I withstand. The very sight of priests, monks, councillors, any one almost, of flies and shadows even, has made me quiver like an aspen. Oftentimes I have thrown down my brushes, cursing, because of my impotent hands. They would give me medicine. There is but one potion for me. They would poison me, no doubt. But I am already dead. O God, the beauty of the world!

* * * * *

'Tis all one ravening horror. And I have worshipped Nature! Fool—fool—fool that I was! It is a Monster with a passion for Death. It is a Creature, devouring, insatiable. We are but the froth blown for a moment above its churning jaws.

* * * * *

Is there anything more beautiful than a windless midsummer eve, within the hour of moonrise? Nothing stirs, save the flittering bats. The slow-circling fireflies swing their flames among the cypress boughs. Nature is dead, or asleep. God leans downward wistfully, and looks betwixt the stars of His azure veil upon the world the foolish priests say is His. Somewhere in the unsunned gyres of infinity, the unknown God, the third and conquering Protagonist, looks upward, with dim prevision, beyond the twin Portals of his Rest—Oblivion and Chaos.

* * * * *

(Appended in the Script of Messer Antonio del Monte, Chemist and Naturalist, of Florence.)

Yester-morn, not having seen the maestro for many days, and knowing how his madness has been growing upon him, I went through his desolate garden, strewn with the bones of the many rare beasts and what not he hath purchased from me, and ruinous with decay and damp vicious glooms, and then up the broken marble stairs to his door. There was a weight against it. I pushed it to, and lo, the corpse of Piero, with a most awful horror on its face, lying head towards me, with the feet still upon the stairway. I note this here at once, lest any questioning should arise. Here, also, I record his own wish, told me but a half-month ago, that he was to be buried in his garden, betwixt a great heavy iron crucifix that would cover him, and an equally huge and heavy iron cross. Upon the former was to be engraved the single word, SPES, upon the latter, NATURA.

(Requiescat in Pace: Antonio Barili del Monte.)

THE BIRTH, DEATH, AND RESURRECTION OF A TEAR

To A. C.

THE BIRTH, DEATH, AND RESURRECTION OF A TEAR

It is not only the haschisch eater who can, in a moment, pass from the exigent life of the commonplace to the dear tyranny of dreams. How trivial, how laboriously methodical, is that vulgar approach to pleasure—the pipe of the opium-smoker, or the drugged coffee of the slave of Indian hemp.

There is another avenue to the gate of dreams. Those who have the secret may enter at any moment from the maze of life and move swiftly to the goal: more swift than the desert mare, the fleetfoot wind.

Thus it was, that to-day, when amid ordinary surroundings, and alone with a dear friend to whom I had come to say farewell—a word unsaid after all, and this because of a dream—I was suaded from myself by one of those unexpected visionary reveries which relieve even the weariest days of the dreamer.

It was not willingly I had gone to see my friend. My love for her had grown too bitter, and at last I had come to believe that she was of a hard and cynical spirit. But for my own sake, as well as for what lay beyond, I determined to make an end of what was become intolerable. Nor was I allured from my purpose by her beauty, her grace, her exquisitely restrained cordiality. The bitterness of renunciation, the greater bitterness of a conviction that she felt only with the brain and the nerves, and not with the heart, restrained me.

We had talked of many things of no real moment, and yet I was no nearer what I had to say. I remembered the words of a friend who also had loved her, and loved vainly: "She is beautiful as the sea, and as cold, as emotionless, as deadly cruel."

I know not by what accident it was that, as she stooped over the silver tea-tray, which caught the vagrant glow of the fire—all of light and sound there was in that quietude of dusk—a sparkle as of a diamond came from behind the long dark eyelashes which so greatly enhanced her beauty. It was an unshed tear;

for I saw it glimmer like a dewdrop amid twilight shadows, then suspend tremulously. Yet it did not fall at last down that lovely sunbrown cheek no bloom of any " sun'd September apricock" could outvie : as dew it came and was absorbed again.

Whether the dear surprise, or the mere white glimmer of that errant herald from the heart, fascinated me, I know not; but suddenly my mind was in that motionless suspension which the windhover has when she lifts her breast against a sudden tide of air.

I saw before me, and far behind, a lustrous expanse of waters. The sun-dazzle was upon those nearest to me, and the wind, frothing the little gold and silver cups tossed continuously by the blue wavelets, made a sunny laughter for leagues amid the yellow-meaded prairies of azure. Beyond, the saffron shimmer lay upon hyacinthine hollows deepening to limitless spaces of purple. Then the sky-line and the sea-line met, and blue within blue was lost.

I had scarce apprehended the vast extent, the near witching beauty, when I realised that I was submerged in fathomless depths. I had not fallen, and had no sense of falling: rather, without sound or motion, the depths had invisibly expanded, and now enfolded me.

So wrought by wonder was I, that when I saw a green lawn stretching before me I did not know whether to advance or to look upon it as one of the fluid lawns of the sea. Then I reflected that in the depths the sea-water would not be of a sunlit green. The next moment I was walking swiftly across it, and I remember how soft and springy was the turf beneath my feet.

All sense of the marvellous had now left me. When, overhead, I heard the rapturous song of lark after lark, I was no more astonished. Why should I be, when my eyes were filled with the beauty of the wild-roses which fell in veils over the wilding hedges and almost hid the honeysuckle and fragrant briar: when every sense was charmed by the loveliness of each garth and copse I passed on my way into a woodland, in whose recesses I could hear the cooing of doves and the windy chimes of cascades and singing brooks?

Never had I seen any forest so beautiful. As I advanced, the trees had an aspect of ancient grandeur, or of a loveliness which went to my heart. Avenue after avenue, vista after vista, disclosed innumerable perspectives of green foliage and the hues of a myriad flowers, with golden sunlight breaking everywhere, and overhead and between the high boughs a sky of a deep joy-giving blue. White birds, and others rainbow-hued, drifted through the sun-warm spaces or flashed from branch to branch. The fern quivered every here and there with the leaping of the fawns, the bleating of the does audible the while by some unseen watercourse. Some of the flowers were familiar: wild hyacinth and windflowers, orchis and the purple anemone, kingcups and daffodils, and many others, all children of the Spring, but otherwise without heed of their wonted season, so that the primrose and the wild-rose were neighbours, and snowdrops and aconites clustered under the red hawthorn.

But there were also others which were strange. Many of these seemed to me as though rubies and emeralds and rainbow-hued opals had risen from their rocky beds in the depths of the earth, and stolen to the surface, and bared their breasts to the kisses of the sunflame which gave them life and joy even while it consumed them with its passionate ardour.

The birds, too, were wonderful to behold. There were among them what seemed blooms of pink or azure fire with wings of waving light: and the song of these was so wilderingly sweet that Ecstasy and Silence, walking hand in hand through that Eden of Dream, knew not when they became one, the Joy that cannot be seen nor uttered nor divined.

Through all this loveliness I went as one wrought by the gladness of death. Some such rapture as this must oftentimes allure the liberated soul when, the veil rent, the air of a new and stronger delight is inhaled at every breath.

Then, all at once, I knew I was not alone in that lovely Avalon. Voices of surpassing sweetness prevailed through the green branches. I thought at first that the whispering leaves were the sighs and laughter of the happy dead. One haunting sweet voice I followed, a delicate, remote, exquisite ululation, faint as dream-music across the dark sea of sleep. Like one winged I went, for the trees slid motionlessly by, as, to the wind, they must seem to recede from his lifting pinions.

In the very inmost Eden of that paradise I stood at last, silent, intent. Beside a fount, whose crystalline wave was filled with sun-gold

RESURRECTION OF A TEAR

and frothed with sun-dazzle, bent a spirit of a loveliness of which I cannot speak. She was as though she were a beam of light from the places, east of the sun and west of the moon, where the young seraphim for joy reweave the perishing rainbows.

About her were beautiful tremulous phantoms, coming and going, appearing and vanishing. These were joys and hopes, aspirations and unspoken prayers, dear desires and longings and wistful yearnings, fair thoughts and delicate dreams.

From her I looked into that halcyon water. The sparkle, the shine of it, entranced me.

At last I spoke. She turned, glanced at me with a shy, sweet serenity, and, after a brief incertitude, beckoned to me to approach.

I knew that I had never looked upon any one so lovely; yet, her face was vaguely familiar. Doubtless it was Ideala, long sought, long dreamed of.

"Look," she whispered, as soon as she had slipped her hand into mine. Together we bent over the sunlit fount. It was like an opal in its lovely hues. In the very core of it I saw what seemed the most exquisite pearl. This appeared to me to be forming, for every moment it grew lovelier. Suddenly it rose, came to the surface, and, for a few seconds, was filled with sunlight, before it welled into one of the many golden conduits which, I now noticed, led from the fountain.

A few seconds: yet in that single pulse of time I learned a wonderful thing. "Do you see this fount?" said Ideala again, in the same low thrilling whisper: "it is the heart of my heart."

"Of your heart, O beautiful Dream?"

"Yes. Do you not know that you are now in my heart? All this fair Eden you have traversed, since you came from the deep wave that brought you hither, is my heart. You saw the flowers, you heard the songs of the birds, the voice of cool waters, the murmur of strange winds: Did none interpret to you?

"And all these lovely phantoms, these beautiful Hopes and Aspirations and tender Sympathies and brave Heroisms?"

"They are my helpers and servers; but I do not see them."

"And this fount, this sunlit water?"

"It is the Fount of Tears that is in every woman's heart. Now it is warmed with flooding sunshine, because I love. Thus it is that the tears that rise are single just now: and are so beautiful, wrought as they are of rainbow-hope."

"And who are you?" I cried, a sudden, wild, passionate hope coming upon me like a tempest, making me as a leaf before the wind.

She looked at me amazedly.

Her lips moved, but I caught no sound. A swift mist was rising between us. She had withdrawn her hand, and though eagerly I stretched my arms I could not reach her.

A name, the dearest of all names, burst from my lips. I saw a wonderful light in the beautiful face. The eyes, the eyes told me all. Lamps of home, sweet lamps of home!

There was a rush of waters. The tear I had seen welling from her heart was the same as that which died on her eyes, and had in its death borne me to the lovely sanctuaries of her heart. Again, it expanded into a great wave; again a limitless ocean stretched beyond me; again I was enveloped and borne swiftly from depth below to depth above, till the senses for one flashing second reeled as the soul returned from its moment's flight.

Did I say an unshed tear gleamed upon me from behind the dark eyelashes of her whom I loved, and so little understood, so scarcely knew?

Truly, I saw it glimmer like a dewdrop amid twilight shadows: then suspend tremulously: but now—how long ago, or but the breath of a moment?—that which had been borne in longing and had died in pain, knew, now, a lovely resurrection.

My heart was full of a great joy, a great reverence. I rose, trembled, and at that moment the tear fell down the lovely sunbrown cheek no bloom of any "sun'd September apricock" could outvie.

THE SISTER OF COMPASSION

To A. M. C.

THE SISTER OF COMPASSION

THE June sunshine moved upon me like a flood. In my sleep, or drowsy reverie, as I lay in the hollow of the tamarisk-fringed dunes which formed the frontier between the forest and the sea, I could hear the two most thrilling voices of Nature—the murmur of a slow wind meshed among green branches, and the confused whispered tumult of great waters.

The unwontedly sustained crying of a gull caused me to stir, turn, and lean on my elbows, with my face against the near waving of the birches which ran out from the woodland. A score of yards to the right, a boulder rose from a garth of fern. Its forehead was white with bleached sea-moss, its sides golden with lichen; and like a white magnolia-bloom upon it was a snowy fulmar, crouching in pain. I saw that the poor bird had been wounded, and as it attempted to rise, at the moment I stirred, I could see that it had been shot, for the left wing was helplessly adroop.

If the fulmar would let me approach, I believed I could ease its agony; but, alas, man is the apparition of Death to his weaker comrades in the common heritage of life. By his own madness of wrong and cruelty he has forfeited that elder brotherhood which should be his pride as it is natively his right.

How, indeed, as it was through the wanton act of a man that the bird had been given over to prolonged agony and sure death, could it have been otherwise; yet it was with deep disappointment that, after I had been allowed to approach within a few yards' distance, the fulmar suddenly hurled itself into the fern. There, like a wounded duck among sedge and bulrush, it floundered heavily in a wild and despairing panic.

From the sky, a living blue, came the songs of unseen larks: from the woodland, the cooing of cushats, the sweet chitter of small birds, the blithe notes of throstle and mavis: from the sea, the chime of green wavelets running up foamy channels or leaping along among the shallows, and, beyond, that deep mysterious rhythm that contains the pulse of Time. Peace brooded upon sky, and sea, and land; but, like a laugh from hell heard among the alleys of paradise, the screaming of the wounded gull turned the sweet savour of life into bitterness.

It was at this moment I became aware of a rumour in the forest. From beech and chestnut, from lime and tall elm, from scyamore and hazel, came a ripple of sweet notes, a rustle of wings. The beech-mast crackled with the scurrying of rabbits. Young foxes, wood-hares, squirrels, stirred through the bracken round the great-rooted oaks. Across the dry water-course the shrew-mice pattered.

It was not consternation, for there were no startled cries, no reckless flight. The jay screamed no warning; the single snapping bark of the fox was unheard.

Suddenly I stood as though entranced. I saw a woman, clothed in white, moving through the sun-splashed woodland. So radiant was the warm white of her robe, that the leaf and branch-shadows, trailing on the golden light that overlay the moss, seemed pale blue.

Through the branches over her head a myriad company of birds hovered, from the wandering cuckoo to the shy ringdove, from the misselthrush to the wren. I saw the falcon flying harmlessly among the chaffinches, and a windhover moving unheeded among the crowd of fluttering sparrows.

Around, and behind her, were animals of all kinds. By her side, wild fawns, stretching their long necks towards her, blessed her with the unconscious benediction of their eyes. One small fawn was dappled red as with autumnal leaves, or as with blood. It moved by her right, and seemed to live only by the love and pity wherewith she sustained it, by healing hand or caressing touch. In her breast was a spot of dull red. I thought it was blood, but it was only a wounded robin which she had rescued from the snare of the bird-trapper. It slept against the warmth of her bosom : its tiny pulse of life lifting the small ruddy breast in rhythm with the larger rise and fall.

The woman was young, in the beautiful youth of those who are not of this world. On her face, fair with charity, sweet with lovingkindness, there was the trouble of something unfulfilled. Her eyes, which mirrored the passionate tenderness of her heart, were intent upon somewhat I could not see: some goal within the sunlit greenery, beyond the dim vistas of misty light, of verdurous gloom; or, perhaps, upon horizons I could not discern.

I should have taken her for a vision, a spirit, but that I saw how womanly sweet she was. The white soul within her was known of every dumb or dwarfed soul among those glad bondagers of her spell, from the falcon to the timid rabbits which leaped before her way like living surf. Moreover, she could see and hear what mortal eyes and ears could; for suddenly she caught sight of the dying gull. Swift as a wave she was beside it. With deft hands she eased the broken wing: with gentle touch she stilled the fierce pulsation. The bird looked upon her as he might have scanned a sunlit sea. A new light came into his eyes: a thrill shook his now elastic body; and though death darkened his life, the spirit which had animated him was set free, and was borne seaward by the wind.

As she rose, for she had kneeled to lay the white body where the swift chemistry of air and light would work the wise corruption of the lifeless into new life, I recognised the face.

She was one whom I had loved and honoured, whom I love and honour: a woman so wrought by the tragic pain of the weak and helpless, that, like one whom she followed blindly from afar, she daily laid down her life in order that she might be as balm here, and here might save, and at all times and in all places be a messenger of that tardy redemption which man must make in spirit and deed for the incalculable wrong which he has done to that sacred thing he most values—Life.

I know not now what that sea was, where that forest is. But I dream, O Sister of Compassion, what was the mysterious voice of the one whispered in your ears, what the confused murmur of the other echoed in your heart.

I know not, but I dream; and I think the forest is that dark wood of human life, that *silva oscura* of living death or dying life which Dante saw with deep awe: and the sea, that ocean of mystery which involves us with a regenerating air, with a life that is not our own, with horizons of promise, and dim perspectives of inalienable hope.

And you, dear friend, are you one whom I and others have known and loved; or had I but a vision of the elect of the Following Love? Where is the goal you hungered for with those intent eyes, O Sister of Compassion,: what the end, and whither the way?

THE HILL-WIND

To F. M.

THE HILL-WIND

WHEN the Hill-Wind awoke by the tarn the noontide heats were over. The blithe mountain-air, fragrant with thyme and honey-ooze, with odours of pine and fir, flowed softly across the uplands. The sky was of a deep, lustrous, wind-washed azure, turquoise-tinct where it caught the sun-flood southerly and westerly. A few snowy wisps of vapour appeared here and there, curled like fantastic sleighs or sweeping aloft as the tails of wild horses; then quickly became attenuated, or even all at once and mysteriously disappeared. Far and near the grouse called, or rose from the cranberry-patches in the ling in their abrupt flurries of flight, beating the hot air with their pinions till it was vibrant with the echoing whirr. The curlews wheeled about the water-courses, crying plaintively. Faint but haunting sweet as remote chimes, the belling of the deer was audible in the mountain-hollows.

A myriad life thrilled the vast purple upland. The air palpitated with the innumerable suspirations of plant and flower, insect and bird and beast. Curious in the tarn the speckled trout caught the glint of the wandering sunray; far upon the heights the fleeces of the small hill-sheep seemed like patches of snow in the sunlight; remote on the scaur beyond the highest pines, the eagle, as he stared unwaveringly upon the wilderness beneath him, shone resplendent as though compact of polished bronze set with gems.

Every sound, every sight, was part of the intimate life of the Hill-Wind. All was beautiful: real. The remote attenuated scream of the eagle: the high thin cry of the kestrel when doubling upon herself in hawking the moorland: the floating lilt of the yellow-hammer: the air-eddies sliding through the honey-laden spires of heather, or whispering among the canna and gale: the myriad murmur from the leagues of sunswept ling and from the dim grassy savannahs which underlay that purple roof: each and all were to her as innate voices.

For a long time she lay in a happy suspension of all thought or activity, fascinated by the reflection of herself in the tarn. Lovely was the image. The soft, delicately-rounded white limbs, the flower-like body, seemed doubly white against the wine-dark purple of the bell-heather and the paler amethyst of the ling. The large shadowy eyes, like purple-blue pansies, dreamed upward from the face in the water. Beautiful as was the sun-dazzle in the hair that was about her head as a glory of morning, even more beautiful was the shimmer of gold and fleeting amber shot through the rippled surface and clear-brown undercalm of the tarn; where also was mirrored, with a subtler beauty than above, the tremulous sulphur-butterfly, poising its yellow wings as it clung to her left breast, ivory-white, small, and firm.

Dim inarticulate thoughts passed through the mind of the Oread—for an Oread the Hill-Wind had been, long, long ago, beyond many lovely transformations—as she lay dreaming by the mountain-pool. Down what remote avenues of life fared her pilgrim eyes, seeking ancestral goals; from what immemorial past arose, like flying shadows at dawn, recollections of the fires of sunrise kindling along the mountain-summits, of the flames of sunset burning slowly upward from the beech-forests to the extreme pines, sombre torches erelong against the remotest snows; vague remembrances of bygone pageants of day and night, of the voicing of old-world winds and the surpassing wonder of the interchange and outgrowth of the seasons, from the Spring Chant of the Equinox to the dirge Euroclydon. Ever and again drifted through her mind fleeting phantoms of life still nearer to herself: white figures, seen in vanishing glimpses of unpondered, all-unconscious reverie —figures which slipt from tree to tree in the high hill-groves, or leaped before the wind, with flying banners of sunlit hair, or stooped to drink from the mountain-pools which the deer forsook not at their approach. Who, what, was this white shape, upon whose milky skin the ruddy light shone, as he stood on a high ledge at sundown and looked meditatively upon the twilit valleys and gloomsome underworld far below? Whose were these unremembered yet familiar sisters, flowerlike in their naked beauty, gathering moonflowers for garlands, while their straying feet amid the dew made a silver shimmer as of gossamer-webs by the waterfalls? Who was the lovely vision, so like that mirrored in the tarn before her, who, stooping in the evergreen-glade to drink the moonshine-dew, suddenly lifted her head, listened intently, and smiled with such wild shy joy?

What meant those vague half-glimpses, those haunting illusive reminiscences of a past that was yet unrememberable?

Troubled, though she knew it not, unconsciously perplexed, vaguely yearning with that nostalgia for her ancestral kind which had been born afresh and deeply by the contemplation of her second self in the mountain pool, the Hill-Wind slowly rose, stretched her white arms, with her hands spraying out her golden hair, and gazed longingly into the blue haze beyond.

Suddenly she started, at the irruption of an unfamiliar sound that was as it were caught up by the wind and flung from corrie to corrie. It was not like the fall of a boulder, and it sounded strangely near. Stooping, she plucked a sprig of gale: then, idly twisting it to and fro, walked slowly to where a mountain-ash, ablaze with scarlet berries, leaned forward from a high heathery bank overlooking a wide hollow in the moors. A great dragon-fly spun past her like an elf's javelin. The small yellow-brown bees circled round and brushed against her hair, excited by this new and strange flower that moved about like the hill-sheep or the red deer. As she stood under the shadow of the rowan and leaned against its gnarled trunk, two small blue butterflies wavered up from the heather and danced fantastically over the sun-sprent gold above her brow. She laughed, but frowned as a swift swept past and snapt up one of the azure dancers. With a quick gesture she broke off a branch of the rowan, but by this time the other little blue butterfly had wavered off into the sunlight.

Holding the branch downward she smiled as she saw the whiteness of her limbs beneath the tremulous arrowy leaves and the thick clusters of scarlet and vermilion berries. Whenever the gnats, whirling in aerial maze, came too near, she raised the rowan branch and slowly waved them back. Suddenly . . . her arm stiffened, and she stood motionless, rigid, intent. It was the Voice of the Sea, the dull, obscure, summoning voice that whispered to the ancient Gods, and called and calls to all Powers and Dominions that have been and are; the same that is in the ears of Man as an echo; and in the House of the Soul as a rumour of a coming hour.

Motionless herself, her eyes travelled through the long haze-blue vistas of the hills. The scythe-swift Shadow of a mighty pinion moved from slope to slope. The Hill-Wind sighed. Then, smiling under some new impulse of joy, she leaped forward, but only indolently to throw herself upon a flood of sunlight streaming by.

The wide reach of harebell-waters, beyond where the heather broke down to the sea, shimmered suddenly into a dazzle of gold flame. A few waves swung aloft their coronals of foam, laughing joyously to the chant of their sweet sea-tune. They had gained a sister: the Sea-wind, a bride: and Ocean a breath, a suspiration, an ended sigh.

LOVE IN A MIST

To a Midsummer Memory

LOVE IN A MIST

IN a green hollow in the woodlands, Love, a mere child, with sunny golden curls and large blue eyes, stood whimpering. A round tear had fallen on his breast and trickled slowly down his white skin, till it lay like a dewdrop on his thigh: another was in pursuit, but had reached no further than a dimple in the chubby cheek, into which it had heedlessly rolled and could not get out again. Beside Love was a thicket of white wild roses, so innumerable that they seemed like a cloud of butterflies alit on a hedge for a moment and about to take wing—so white that the little wanderer looked as though he were made of rose-stained ivory. Here was the cause of the boy's whimpering. A thorn-point had slightly scratched his right arm, barely tearing the skin but puncturing it sufficiently to let a tiny drop of blood, like a baby rowan-berry, slowly well forth.

Love looked long and earnestly at the wound. Then he whimpered, but stopped to smile at a squirrel who pretended to be examining the state of its tail, but was really watching him. When the little drop of blood would neither roll away nor go back, Love grew angry, and began to cry.

"Ah, I am so weak," he sighed; "perhaps I shall die! Ah, wretched little soul that I am, to lie here in this horrible thorny wood. No—no—I will drag myself out into the sunshine, and die there. Perhaps—p'raps—(*sniffle*)—'aps—(*sniffle*)—a kind lark will"—(*sniffle*).

Sobbing bitterly, Love crept through a beech-hedge, and so into the open sunlit meadow beyond. He was so unhappy that he quite forgot to knock off from a grey thistle a huge snail, although its shell shone temptingly many-hued; and even a cricket that jumped on to his foot and then off again hardly brought to his face a wan smile.

But after sitting awhile by a heavy burdock, and sobbing at gradually lengthening intervals, he stopped abruptly. Out of a garth of red clover and white campions he saw two round black eyes staring at him with such unmitigated astonishment that he could do nothing else but stare back with equal rigidity and silence.

"Why, it is only a brown hare," exclaimed Love below his breath. "How it smiles!"—and therewith he broke into so hearty a laugh that the hare sprang round as if on a pivot, and went leaping away through the meadow. Beyond the puffed campions were a cluster of tall oxe-eye daisies, and they moved so temptingly towards him in the breeze that Love ran as it were to meet them.

No sooner, however, was he in their midst than he pluckt them one by one, and then ran back with them towards the wood, in whose cool shadow, he thought, it would be delightful to weave of them a starry wreath.

But by the time the wreath was woven, Love was both thirsty and aweary of being still. So, having sipped the dew from a bed of green mosses among the surface-roots of a vast oak, he ran into a little wilderness of wild hyacinths, and danced therein with maddest glee, while the sunlight splashed upon him through the dappling shadows of the oak boughs.

A fat bumble-bee and two white butterflies joined him for a time, but at last the bee grew hot and breathless, and the butterflies were frightened by his joyous laughter and the clapping of his little hands. Scarce, however, was he left alone once more than he descried a young fawn among the fern. It took him but a moment to snatch his wreath of ox-eye daisies, and but another to spring to the side of the startled fawn and place the wreath round its neck. The great brown eyes looked fearfully at Love, who, little rascal, pretended to be caressing when he was really making ready for a leap. In a second he was on the fawn's back —but, ah! poor Love, he had not calculated for such a flight. Away sped the fawn, athwart the glade, through the hollow, and out across the meadow towards the sand-dune. Gradually Love's hold became more and more insecure, and at last off he came right into a mass of yellow irises and a tadpole-haunted little pool.

Love might have stopped to cry, or at least to chase the tadpoles, but he happened to see a sea-gull flying low beyond him across the dunes. With a shout he pursued it, forgetful alike of the fawn and his lost wreath.

But when he came to the break in the dunes he could not see the ocean because of the haze that lay upon it, and in which the sea-gull was soon lost to sight. But at least the sands were there. For a time he wandered disconsolately along the shore. Then, when he saw the tide slowly advancing, he frowned. "Ha! ha!" he laughed, "I shall build a castle of sand, and then the sea will not know what to do, and the white gull will come back again."

But having built his sand-castle, Love was so weary that he curled himself up behind the shallow barrier, and, having wearily but lovingly placed beside him three pink half-shells, a pearly willie-winkie, a piece of wave-worn chalk, and a hermit-crab (which soon crawled away), he was speedily asleep.

Before long the ripple of the water against the very frontier of his small domain aroused the brine-bred things that live by the sea-marge. A few cockles gaped thirstily, and one or two whistle-fish sent their jets of water up into the air and then protruded their shelly shouts as if to scan the tardy advance of the tide. The sand-lice bestirred themselves, creeping, leaping, confusedly eager not to be overtaken by that rapid ooze which would quicksand them in a moment.

Then a piece of dulse was washed right on to the castle-wall. On the salt-smelling wrack was a crab, and this startled voyager saw dry land and mayhap new food to sample in the white foot of Love that lay temptingly near. Just then a flying shrimp, a mad aeronaut, a reckless enthusiast among its kind, took the fortress at a leap and alighted on Love's white and crinkled belly. The boy's body instinctively shivered. Still, he might not have awaked, had not the crab at that moment joyously gripped, as succulent prey, his little toe, curled as it was like a small and dainty mollusc.

Love sat up, and with indignant eyes remonstrated with the crab, who had at once given way and retreated with haphazard assiduity to the shelter of a convenient pebble partially embedded in the sand.

As for the shrimp, it had come and gone like the very ghost of a tickle, like the dream-fly of sleepland.

But suddenly Love heard a voice, a low whisper, coming he knew not whence, and yet so strangely familiar. Was it borne upon the white lips of the tide, or did it come from the curving billow that swept shoreward, or from the deep beyond? Who can guess what the voice said, since Love himself knew not the sweet strange word, but was comforted: knowing only that he was to return to the wood again. Fragments he caught, though little comprehensible: "My child, my little wandering Love, who art born daily, and art ever young," and then the words of which he knew nothing, or but vaguely apprehended.

Yet ever petulant, Love would rather have stayed by the sea, even to the undoing of his castle-walls, already toppling with the upward reaching damp of the stealthy underooze, had he not descried a white wild-goat standing on the dune and looking at him with mild eyes like sunlit sardonyx. With a glad cry he ran towards the goat, who made no play of caprice but seemed to invite, for all the strangeness of the essay, this young rider with the child's smile and the emperor's eyes.

The yellow-hammers and ousels, the whinchats and sea-larks sent abroad long thrilling notes in their excitement, as the white goat, with Love laughingly astride, raced across the dunes and over the meadows towards the wood. But as the too-impulsive steed took a fallen oak at a bound, its feet caught in the loose bark, and poor Love was shot forward into a hollow of green moss. Alas, in the comet-like passage thither, a nettle slightly stung the sole of one foot; so that the moment he had recovered from his somersault he snatched a broken oak-branch, and turned to chastise the too heedless goat. But, to his astonishment, no goat was to be seen. It had disappeared as though it were a blossom blown by the wind.

Rubbing his eyes, Love looked again and again. No goat; no sound, even, save the ruffling of the low wind among the lofty domes of the forest, the tap-tapping of a woodpecker, the shrill cry of a jay and indiscriminate warbling undertone of a myriad birds, with, below all, the chirp of the grasshopper and the drone of the small wood-wasp and the foraging bee.

Beyond the last copse the sun was slowly moving in a whirl of golden fire.

Hark! what was that? Love started, and then slipped cautiously from tree to tree, finding his way into the woodland like a gliding sunray. He heard voices, and a snatch of a song:—

> "The wild bird called to me 'Follow!'
> The nightingale whispered 'Stay!'
> When lost in the hawthorn-hollow
> We" . . . . .

The next moment he descried a lovely girl lying on the moss below an oak, with her face towards the setting sun, whose warm flood soaked through the wide green flame of the irradiated leaves. A little way beyond her was a young man, no other than the singer, standing by an easel, and putting the last touches to the canvas upon which he was at work.

Love was curious. He had never seen a picture, and, in fact, he thought the man was probably spreading out something to eat. He, child though he was, was so fearless, that no one could have daunted him, and so natively royal, that no idea even of his being gainsaid troubled his brain.

With great interest he stole alongside the painter. He looked at the canvas dubiously; sniffed it; and then turned away with a gesture of disapproval. He liked the look of the pigments on a palette that lay on the ground, and thought that the man was perhaps no other than he who painted the kingcups and violets and the bells of the hyacinths. But the smell made him sick, and so he stole towards the girl to see what *she* was doing.

It vaguely puzzled him that neither the man nor the girl seemed to be aware of his presence; yet, as Love never troubled to think, the bewilderment was but a shadow of a passing cloud. The girl was beautiful. He loved better to look at her than at any other flower of the forest. Even the blue cornflower, even the hedge-speedwell, had not so exquisite a blue as the dream-wrought eyes into whose unconscious depths he looked long, and saw at last his own image, clear as in deep water. "I wish she would sing," said Love to himself; "that man yonder is no better than a huge bumble-bee." With a mischievous glance he pluckt a tall wind-flower, and gently tickled her with it.

A faint smile, a delicate wave of colour, came into her face. "*Ah, Love! Love!*" she whispered below her breath.

How sweet the words were! With a happy sigh Love cuddled up close to the beautiful girl, and, tired and drowsy, would soon have fallen asleep, had not the heaving of her bosom disturbed him.

"Ah, what a tiresome world it is," exclaimed Love fretfully, as he crawled indolently away, and then rested again among some blue flowers. There he sat for some time, sulkily tying a periwinkle round each toe. Suddenly, with a cry of joy, he descried among the flowers his lost bow and sheaf of arrows. With a merry laugh he reached for them, and in mere wantonness began to fray the petals with an arrow, and to tangle them into an intricate net of blue blossom and green fibre.

But in the midst of his glee came retribution. He heard a rustling sound, a quick exclamation, and the next moment an easel fell right atop of him, and, but for his soft, mossy carpet, might have flattened him, for all his white plumpness. True, the easel was picked up again immediately, but Love felt the insult as well as the blow. With a yell of anger, that very nearly startled a neighbouring caterpillar, he fitted an arrow to his bow, and shot it straight at the clumsy owner of the easel. "Aha," he thought, "I have paid you back, you see," for he saw the young man stop, grow pale, hesitate, and then suddenly fall on his knees. "Ah! he is wounded to death," and Love's tender heart got the better of his resentment, and he would fain have recalled that deadly arrow. But to his astonishment the youth seemed more eager to seize and kiss the girl's hand than to save his life, if that were still possible!

As for the girl, the sunset was upon her face as a flame. She tried to rise, and in doing so trampled upon one of Love's toes. Poor little Love danced about furiously on one foot, holding his wounded toe with one hand; but alas!

again his hasty anger overcame him, and, before he realised what he had done, he shot another arrow, this time straight at the heart of the lovely girl.

Alas, how it weakened her at once! In the agony of death, no doubt, she fell forward into the man's arms and laid her head upon his breast.

But speedily Love saw that they were not dead or even dying, but merely kissing and fondling each other, and this too in the most insensate fashion.

"Oh, how funny! how funny!" laughed Love, and rolled about in an ecstasy among the blue flowers, making the tangle worse than ever.

* * * * *

(*Twilight.*)

She. Darling—darling—let me go now—let me go. It will soon be dark.

He. Sweetheart, wait!

She. Hush! What is that?

(*A low tiny snore comes from amidst the blue flowers.*)

He. Oh, it is only a beetle rubbing its shards, or a mole burrowing through the grass.

She. Ah, look; we are trampling under foot such beautiful flowers. These must be *our* flowers, dear, must they not? What are they?

He. I don't know—ah, yes, to be sure—they must be the flower called " Love in a Mist."

She (dreamily). I wonder if we could see Love himself if we searched below all this blue tangle?

. . . She leans down, and peers through the blue veil of the flowers. Love wakes with the fragrance of her warm breath playing upon his cheek, but does not stir, for he is remorseful at having shot an arrow at so lovely a thing. With loving caressing touch he gently lays a dew-drop into each blue flower of her eyes. . . .

She (whisperingly as she rises). How beautiful, how wonderful it all is!

He. Ah, darling, tears in those beautiful eyes! Come, let me kiss them away.

Love (below his breath). Greedy wretch—I gave them to *her!* Ah, she shall have many more, and you, mayhap, none!

Hand in hand, the lovers go away, and, well content, Love turns over on his side and is soon sound asleep. The moon rises, full and golden yellow. From a beech-covert a nightingale sings with intermittent snatches of joy. Above the blue flowers two white night-moths flicker in a slow fantastic wayward dance. A glow-worm, hanging on a lock of Love's curly hair, shines as though it were the child of a moonbeam and a flower.

But at last the glowworm, crawling from its high place and adown the white sweetness of Love's face, tickled his small nose, and caused him to sit up, startled, and wide awake. "What—who?" muttered Love confusedly.

    THE NIGHTJÀR.
Quir-rr-rr-o! . . . *Quir-rr-rr-o!*
    THE NIGHTINGALE.
Kew-u-ēē, kwee! Kwee-kwee-tchug! tchug! tchug! kwee-kwilloh!
   A RESTLESS MAGPIE (*mockingly*).
Kwilloh . . . *kwollow, ohee kwollow-kwan!*
    ECHO.
Follow . . . *oh, follow them!*
    FURTHER ECHO.
Follow! . . . *Fol* . . . *low!*
    LOVE (*rising*).
I come, I come! who calls?
    DISTANT ECHO (*faintly*).
Fol . . . *low.*

www.ingramcontent.com/pod-product-compliance
Lightning Source LLC
Chambersburg PA
CBHW020108170426
43199CB00009B/441